LABORATORY Manual

MATHEMATICS

CBSE Class XI

LABORATORY Manual

MATHEMATICS

CBSE Class XI

Authors
Priyanka Patel, Shikhar Gupta

Name..

Class........................ **Section**...................... **Roll No**......................

School..

arihant
SUCCESS AND NOTHING LESS

Arihant Prakashan (School Division Series)

arihant

SUCCESS AND NOTHING LESS

Arihant Prakashan (School Division Series)

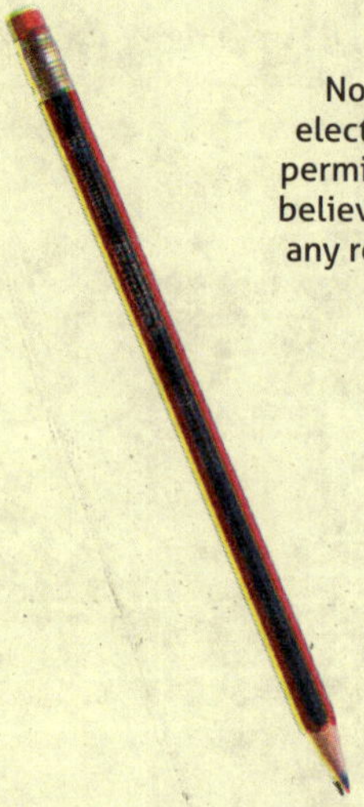

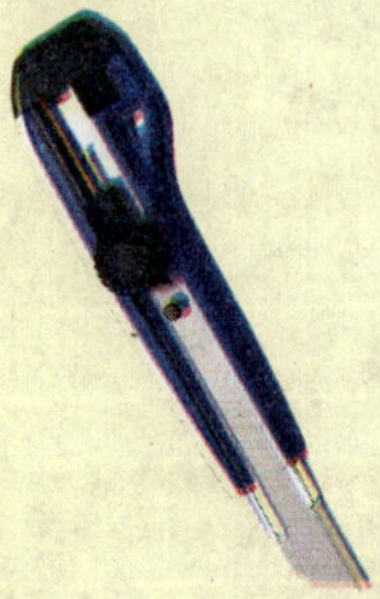

Administrative & Production Offices

Regd. Office

'Ramchhaya' 4577/15, Agarwal Road, Darya Ganj, New Delhi -110002
Tele: 011- 47630600, 43518550; Fax: 011- 23280316

Head Office

Kalindi, TP Nagar, Meerut (UP) - 250002, Tele: 0121-7156203, 7156204

Sales & Support Offices

Agra, Ahmedabad, Bengaluru, Bareilly, Chennai, Delhi, Guwahati, Hyderabad, Jaipur, Jhansi, Kolkata, Lucknow, Nagpur & Pune

Price : ₹350.00

PO No. : TXT-59-T068375-12-25

Published by Arihant Publications (India) Ltd.

For further information about the books from Arihant, log on to **www.arihantbooks.com** or email to **info@arihantbooks.com**

Follow us on

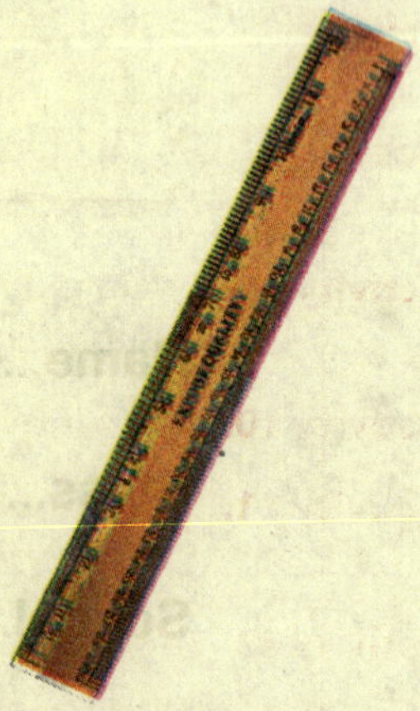

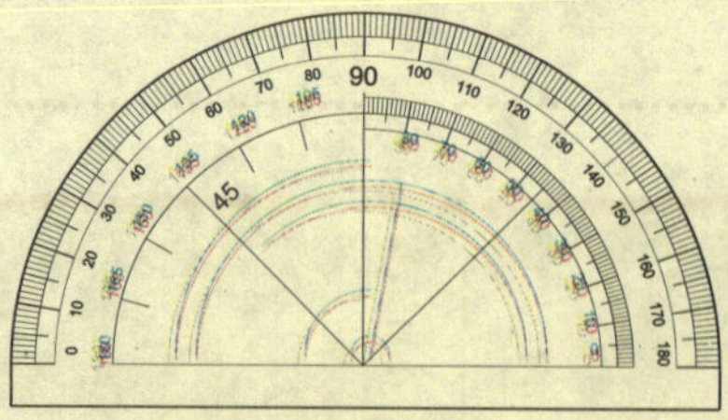

Contents

- The Purpose of The Mathematics Laboratory I
- Role of Mathematics Laboratory in Teaching-Learning II
- Management and Maintenance of Laboratory III
- Materials and Equipments for Mathematics Laboratory IV-V

LIST OF ACTIVITIES

Activity 1.	To verify that for two sets A and B, $n(A \times B) = pq$ and the total number of relations from A to B is 2^{pq}, where $n(A) = p$ and $n(B) = q$.	1-3
Activity 2.	To represent set theoretic operations using Venn diagrams.	4-9
Activity 3.	To verify distributive law for three given non-empty sets A, B and C, that is $A \cup (B \cap C) = (A \cup B) \cap (A \cup C)$	10-11
Activity 4.	To identify a relation and a function.	12-14
Activity 5.	To distinguish between a Relation and Function.	15-16
Activity 6.	To verify the relation between the degree measure and the radian measure of an angle.	17-19
Activity 7.	To find the values of sine and cosine functions in second, third and fourth quadrants using their given values in first quadrant.	20-25
Activity 8.	To prepare a model to illustrate the values of sine function and cosine function for different angles which are multiples of $\frac{\pi}{2}$ and π.	26-28
Activity 9.	To plot the graphs of $\sin x$, $\sin 2x$, $2\sin x$ and $\sin \frac{x}{2}$ using same coordinate axes.	29-31
Activity 10.	To interpret geometrically, the meaning of $i = \sqrt{-1}$ and its integral powers.	32-34
Activity 11.	To find the number of ways in which three cards can be selected from given five cards.	35-37
Activity 12.	To construct a Pascal's Triangle and to write binomial expansion for a given positive integral exponent.	38-40

Activity 13.	To demonstrate that the Arithmetic mean of two different positive numbers is always greater than the Geometric mean.	41-43
Activity 14.	To construct different types of conic sections.	44-48
Activity 15.	To construct a parabola.	49-53
Activity 16.	An alternative method of constructing a parabola.	54-55
Activity 17.	To construct an ellipse using a rectangle.	56-60
Activity 18.	To construct an ellipse with given major and minor axes.	61-62
Activity 19.	To construct an ellipse when two fixed points are given.	63-64
Activity 20.	To explain the concept of octants by three mutually perpendicular planes in space.	65-68
Activity 21.	To find analytically $\lim_{x \to c} f(x) = \frac{x^2-c^2}{x-c}$	69-71
Activity 22.	Verification of the geometrical significance of derivative.	72-76

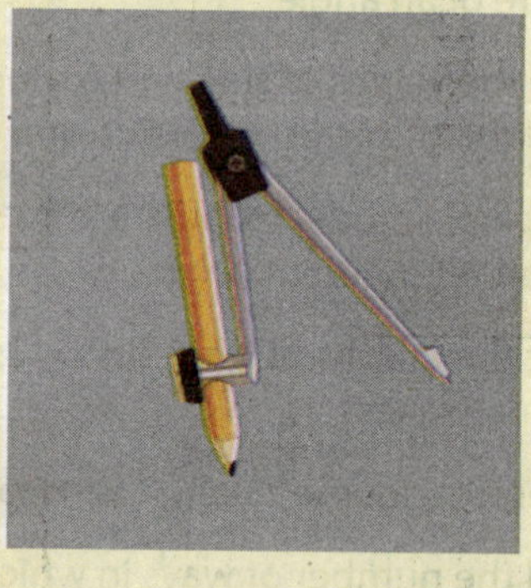

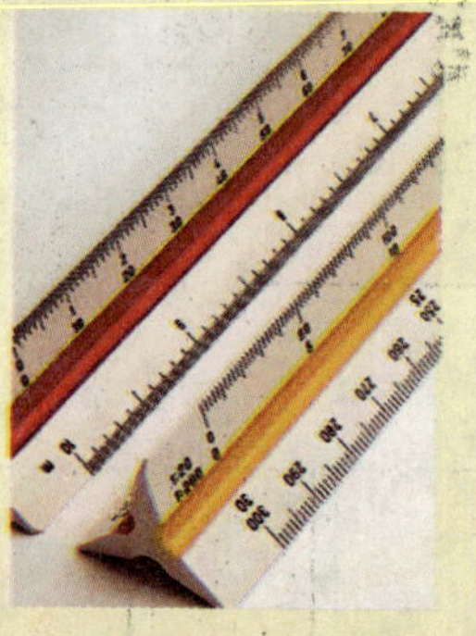
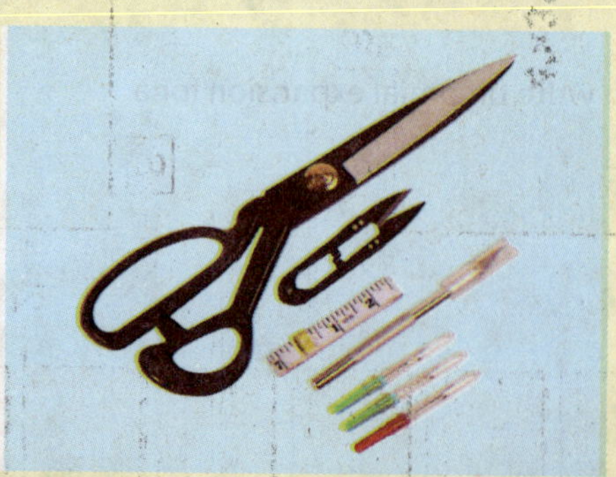

Set-up of Mathematics Laboratory

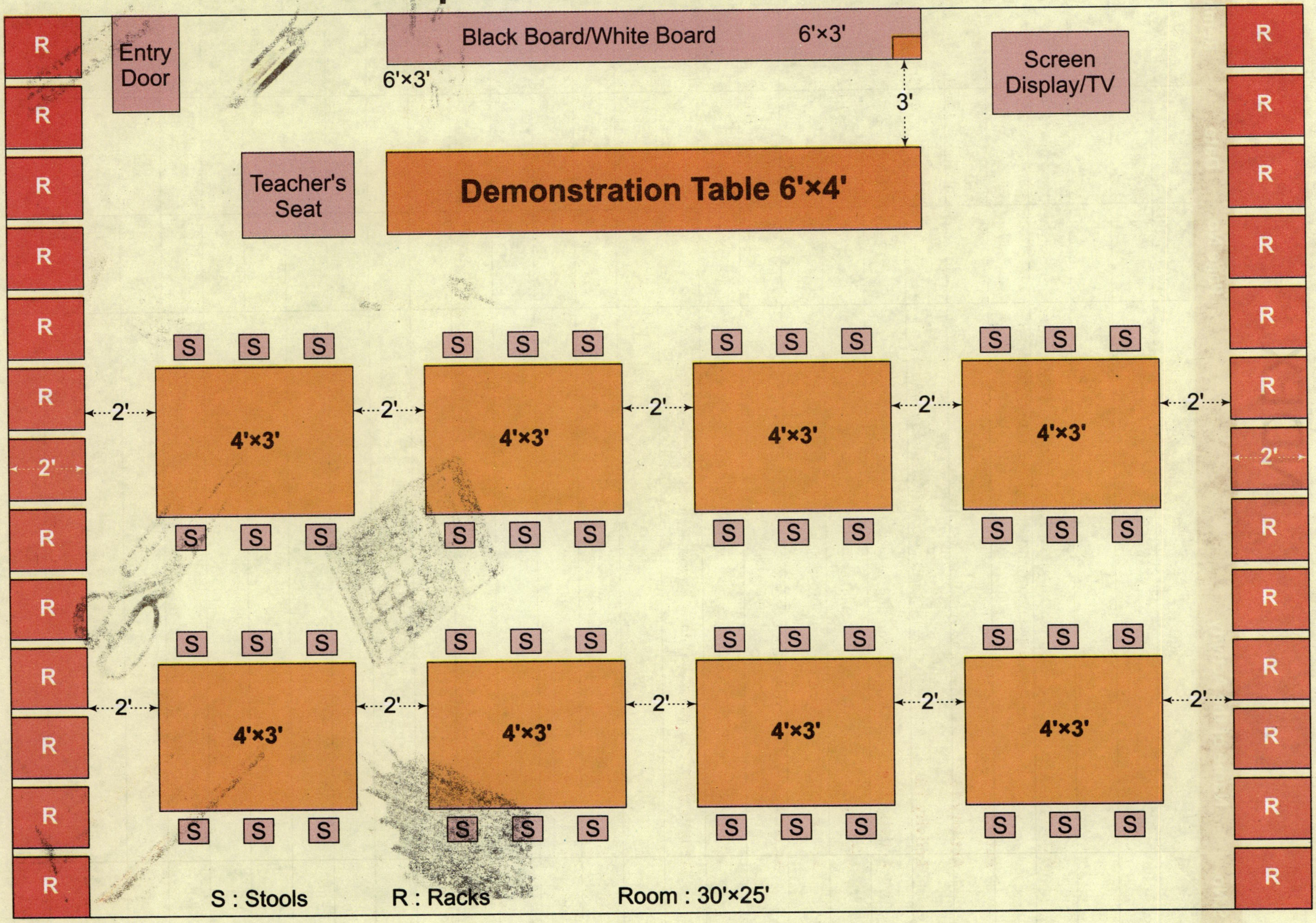

INDEX

S.No.	Name of the Activity	Page No.	Date	Remarks

INDEX

S.No.	Name of the Activity	Page No.	Date	Remarks

INDEX

S.No.	Name of the Activity	Page No.	Date	Remarks

LABORATORY Manual

MATHEMATICS

CERTIFICATE

This is to certify that Activities recorded in this Practical Notebook have been performed

by ______________________________
(Student's name)

of __________ of ______________________________
(class/section) (school name)

during academic session ________________

Examiner Signature	Principal Signature (with school stamp)	Teacher Signature

The Purpose of The Mathematics Laboratory

The main objective of mathematics is to train the students to think and analysis the given situations and act logically. These objectives can only be achieved if there is an opportunity of creating a scope of exploring, verifying and experimenting upon mathematical results by students themselves.

Since, activities create interest among students who wants to explore, and test some of their ideas, beliefs about mathematics and also present a problem or a challenge with the possibility of generating futher challenges and problems. Thus, there is need of adopting activity — oriented process rather than merely concentrating upon mastery of rules and formulae so as to pass out the examinations.

Mathematics laboratory is a place where scientific research and experiments are conducted for verification, exploration or discovery. The role of laboratory is helpful in understanding the mathematical concepts, formulae through activities.

A mathematics laboratory can foster mathematical awareness, skill building, positive attitude and learning by doing experiments in various topics of mathematics such as Algebra, Geometry, Mensuration, Trigonometry, Calculus, Coordinate Geometry, etc. It is the place where students can generate problem and struggle to answer and learn certain concepts using concrete objects and verify many mathematical facts and properties using models, measurements and other activities.

The laboratory will act as a forum for the teachers to discuss and deliberate on some important mathematical issues.

Mathematics laboratory is expected to offer the following opportunities to learners:

- To discover the pattern for getting insight into the formulae
- To visualise algebraic and analytical results geometrically.
- Offers more scope for individual participation. It encourages students to become independent learners.
- To encourage students in recognising, extending, formulating patterns and enabling them to pose problems in the form of conjectures.
- To perform certain recreational activities in mathematics.
- To exhibit relatedness of mathematics with day to day life problems.
- Builds up inherent interest and confidence in the students towards learning and doing mathematics.
- It helps to supplement the knowledge learned in classroom.

Role of Mathematics Laboratory in Teaching-Learning

Mathematics at Senior Secondary stage is a little more abstract as compared to the subject at the secondary stage. The mathematics laboratory at this stage can contribute in a big way to the learning of this subject. Some of the ways are:

- Here the student will get an opportunity to understand the abstract ideas/ concepts through concrete objects and situations.
- The concepts of relations and functions can be easily understood by making working models and by making arrow diagrams using wires.
- Three dimensional concepts can only be conceived by three dimensional models in the laboratory, where as it is very difficult to understand these concepts on a black board.
- The concept of function and its inverse function, becomes very clear by drawing their graphs using mathematical instruments and using the concept of image about the line y=x, which can be done only in the laboratory.
- Since, the larger time available individually to the student and opportunity to repeat an activity several times, students can revise and rethink the problem and solutions. It helps to develop metacognitive abilities.
- It widens the experiential base and lays groundwork for later learning of new areas of mathematics and helps to make approprite connection between the known and unknown in mathematics.

Management and Maintenance of Laboratory

A laboratory is equipped with instruments, apparatus, equipments, models apart from facilities like water, electricity, etc. Non-availability of a single material or facility out of these may hinder the performance of any experiment activity in the laboratory. Therefore, the laboratory must be well managed and well maintained.

Personal Management and Maintenance

In personal management and maintenance following points are considered:

1. **Cleanliness** A laboratory should always be neat and clean. When students perform experiment activities during the day, it certainly becomes dirty and things are scattered. So, it is the duty of the lab staff to clean the laboratory.
2. **Checking and arranging materials for the day's work** Lab staff should know that what activities are going to be performed on a particular day. The material required for the day's activities must be arranged one day before.
3. The facilities like water, electricity, etc. must be checked and made available at the time of experiments.
4. Identify the necessary materials required in the laboratory by labeling them with name tags.
5. Many safety measures are required while working in laboratory. A list of such measures may be pasted on a wall of the laboratory.
6. Electrification of the laboratory should be professionally done to allow for safety use.
7. A first aid kit may be kept in the laboratory.

Management and Maintenance of Materials

To manage and maintain materials for a laboratory following points must be considered:

1. A list of instruments, apparatus, activities and material may be prepared according to the experiments included in the syllabus of mathematics.
2. Arrange the materials in places (on tables, shelves, board, etc) in a way that they can be easily accessed when needed and returned appropriately after use.
3. The instruments, equipments and apparatus should also be checked regularly by the laboratory staff. If any repair is required it should be done immediately.
4. Arrange the benches and tables to allow for free movement in the laboratory.

Materials and Equipments for Mathematics Laboratory

As the students will be involved in a lot of model making activities under the guidance of the teacher, the smooth running of the mathematics laboratory will depend upon the supply of oddments such as strings and threads, cellotape, white cardboard, hardboard, needles and pins, drawing pins, sandpaper, pliers, screwdrivers, rubber bands of different colours, gummed papers and labels, squared papers, plywood, scissors, saw, paint, soldering, solder wire, steel wire, cotton wool, tin and plastic sheets, glazed papers, overhead projector, slide projector, epidiascope, liquid crystal display etc.

Besides these, some models, charts, slides, etc., made up of a good durable material should also be there for the teacher to demonstrate some mathematical concepts, facts and properties before the students. Different tables, ready reckner should also be there (in the laminated form) so that these can be used by the students for different purposes.

In view of the above, following is the list of suggested instruments/models for the laboratory:

Equipment

Mathematical instrument set (Wooden Geometry Box for demonstration containing rulers, set-squares, divider, protractor and compasses), some geometry boxes, metre scales of 100 cm, 50 cm and 30 cm, measuring tape, diagonal scale, clinometer, calculators, computers including related software etc.

Models

For demonstration of

- Sets
- Relations and Functions
- Sine and cosine functions
- Quadratic functions with the help of linear functions
- Complex number
- Principle of mathematical induction
- Sequence and series
- Pascal's triangle
- Arithmetic Progression
- Circle
- Conic Sections
- Limits and Derivatives
- Inequality

- Exponential and logarithmic functions
- Increasing, decreasing functions
- Maxima, minima, point of inflection
- Lagrange's minima, point of inflection
- Rolle's theorem
- Definite Integral as limit of sum
- Angle in semicircle using vectors
- Construction of parabola when distance between directrix and focus is given
- Construction of ellipse when major and minor axes are given
- Octants (In three dimensional space)
- Shortest distance between two skew lines
- Geometrical interpretation of scalar and vector product
- Equation of a straight line passing through a fixed point and parallel to a given vector
- Equation to a plane
- Angle between two planes
- Bisection of the angles between two planes by a third plane
- Intersection of three planes
- Projection of the line segment
- Sample spaces
- Conditional Probability

Activity 1

OBJECTIVE

To verify that for two sets A and B, $n(A \times B) = pq$ and the total number of relations from A to B is 2^{pq}, where $n(A) = p$ and $n(B) = q$.

Material Required

Paper, different coloured pencils.

Prerequisite Knowledge

1. Concept of cartesian product of two sets.
2. Concept of relations.

Method of Construction

1. Take a set A_1, which has one element (say) a_1, and take another set B_1, which has one element (say) b_1.
2. Again, take a set A_2 which has two elements (say) a_1 and a_2, and take another set B_3, which has three elements (say) b_1, b_2 and b_3.
3. Similarly, take a set A_3 which has three elements (say) a_1, a_2 and a_3, and take another set B_4, which has four elements (say) b_1, b_2, b_3 and b_4.

Demonstration

1. After construction, represent all the possible correspondences of the elements of set A_1 to the elements of set B_1 visually as shown in Fig. (1.1)

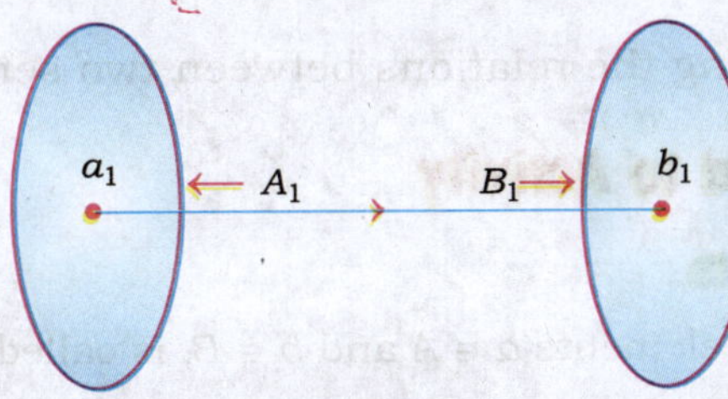

Fig. 1.1

2. Again, represent all the possible correspondences of the elements of set A_2 to the elements of set B_3 visually as shown in Fig. (1.2).

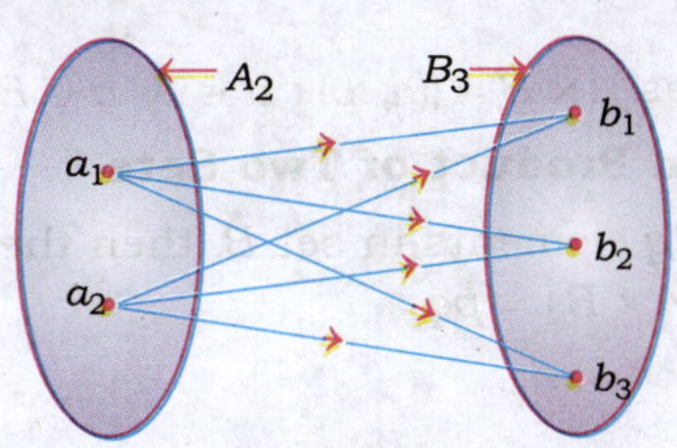

Fig. 1.2

3. Represent all the possible correspondences of the elements of set A_3 to the elements of set B_4 visually as shown in Fig. (1.3)

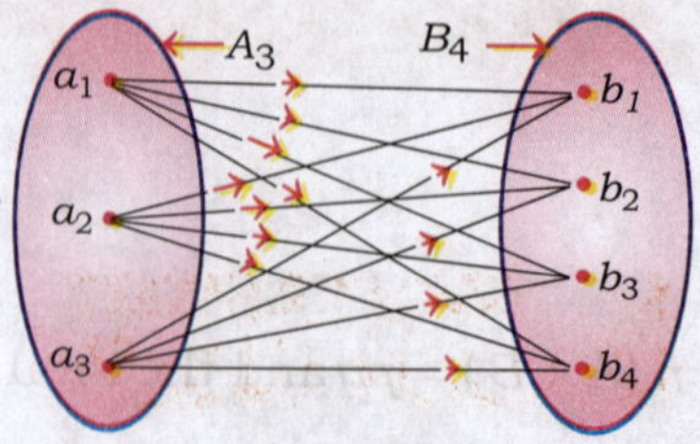

Fig. 1.3

4. In the end of activity, similar visual representations can be shown between the elements of any two given sets A and B.

Observation

1. The number of arrows, i.e. the number of elements in cartesian product $(A_1 \times B_1)$ of the sets A_1 and B_1 is ...×... and the number of relations is $2^{\square}$.
2. The number of arrows, i.e. the number of elements in cartesian product $(A_2 \times B_3)$ of the sets A_2 and B_3 is ...×... and the number of relations is $2^{\square}$.
3. The number of arrows, i.e. the number of elements in cartesian product $(A_3 \times B_4)$ of the sets A_3 and B_4 is ...×... and the number of relations are $2^{\square}$..

Result

We can verify this result by taking other sets $A_4, A_5, \ldots\ldots, A_p$, which have elements 4, 5, ..., p, respectively, and the sets $B_5, B_6 \ldots, B_q$ which have elements 5, 6, ..., q, respectively. More precisely we arrive at the conclusion that in case of given set A containing p elements and the set B containing q elements, the total number of relations from A to B is 2^{pq}, where $n(A \times B) = n(A) \times n(B) = pq$.

Application

We can use this activity for finding the relations between two sets.

Necessary Concepts Related to Activity

1. Cartesian Product of Two Sets

The set of all ordered pairs (a, b) of elements $a \in A$ and $b \in B$, is called the cartesian product of sets A and B and is denoted by $A \times B$.

Or

For two non-empty sets A and B, the cartesian product $A \times B$ is the set of all ordered pairs of elements from sets A and B.

In symbolic form, it can be written as $A \times B = \{(a, b) : a \in A, b \in B\}$

Number of Elements in Cartesian Product of Two Sets

If there are p elements in set A and q elements in set B, then there will be pq elements in $A \times B$, i.e. if $n(A) = p$ and $n(B) = q$, then $n(A \times B) = pq$.

2. Relation

Let A and B be two non-empty sets. Then, a relation R from set A to set B is a subset of cartesian product $A \times B$, i.e. $R \subseteq A \times B$.

Number of Relations

Let A and B be any two non-empty finite sets containing m and n elements, respectively. Then, number of ordered pairs in $A \times B$ is mn.

$\therefore$ Total numbers of subsets of $A \times B$ is 2^{mn}.

Hence, the total number of relations from set A to B is 2^{mn}, because each relation from A to B is a subset of $A \times B$.

Viva-Voce

Q.1 Explain about the cartesian product of two sets.

Ans For two non-empty sets A and B, the cartesian product $A \times B$ is the set of all ordered pairs of elements from sets A and B.

Q.2 What do you mean by 'Relation'?

Ans A relation R from a non-empty set A to a non-empty set B is a subset of cartesian product $A \times B$.

Q.3 If A be a finite set having n elements, then what are the number of relations on set A?

Ans 2^{n^2}

Q.4 Number of relations on A = Number of subsets of $A \times A$. Is it true?

Ans Yes, it is true.

Q.5 If atleast one of A and B is an infinite set and other is a non-empty set, then $A \times B$ is finite set. Is it true or false?

Ans False.

Q.6 If $A = \{1, 2, 3, 4\}$, then how many relation are on A?

Ans $2^{4^2} = 2^{16}$

Q.7 If $A = \{1, 2\}$ and $B = \{3, 4\}$, then total number of relations from A to B is ....

Ans 16

Q.8 'If R_1 and R_2 are two relations from A to B, then $R_1 \cup R_2$, $R_1 \cap R_2$ and $R_1 - R_2$ are also relations from A to B.' Is it true?

Ans Yes, it is true.

Q.9 If $n(A) = p$, $n(B) = q$ and $n(C) = r$, then number of elements in $n(A \times B \times C)$ is ....

Ans pqr

Q.10 If A and B are two non-empty sets having n elements in common, then how many common elements in both $A \times B$ and $B \times A$?

Ans n^2.

Activity 2

OBJECTIVE

To represent set theoretic operations using Venn Diagrams.

Material Required

Cardboard, white thick sheets of paper, different coloured pencil, scissors, gum.

Prerequisite Knowledge

1. Universal set.
2. Concept of Venn diagrams.
3. Concept of operations on sets.

Method of Construction

1. Firstly, cut rectangular strips from a sheet of paper and paste them on a cardboard. Write the symbol U in the left/right top corner of each rectangle.
2. After that, draw two circles A and B each inside of the rectangular strips and shade/colour different portions as shown in Fig. (2.1) to Fig. (2.10).

Demonstration

1. U denotes the universal set represented by the rectangle.
2. Circles A and B represent the subsets of the universal set U as shown in the Fig. (2.1) to Fig. (2.10).
3. A' and B' denote the complement of the set A and set B, respectively as shown in the Fig. (2.3) and Fig. (2.4).
4. In the Fig. (2.1), shaded portion represents $A \cup B$.

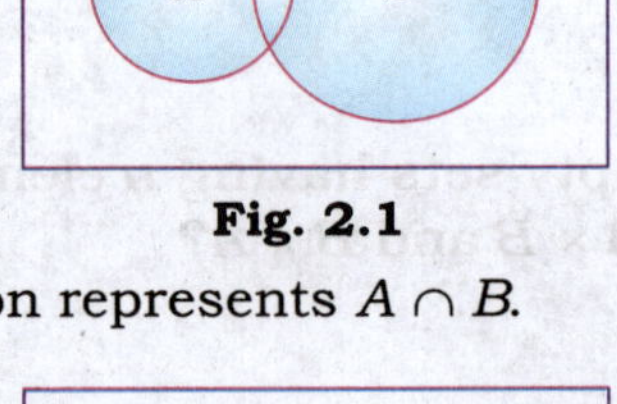

Fig. 2.1

5. In the Fig. (2.2), shaded portion represents $A \cap B$.

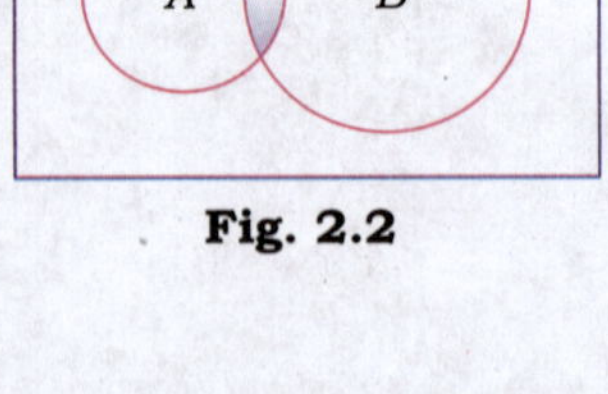

Fig. 2.2

6. In the Fig. (2.3), shaded portion represents A'.

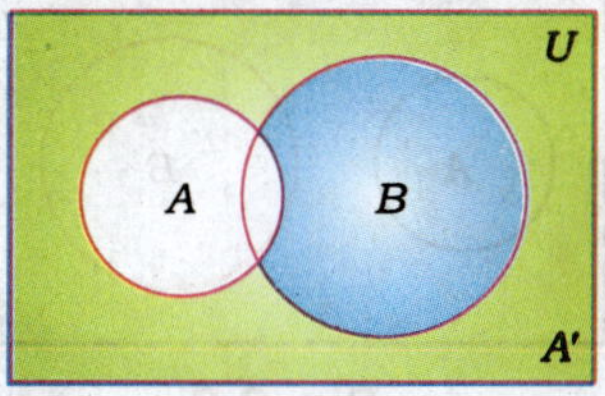

Fig. 2.3

7. In the Fig. (2.4), shaded portion represents B'.

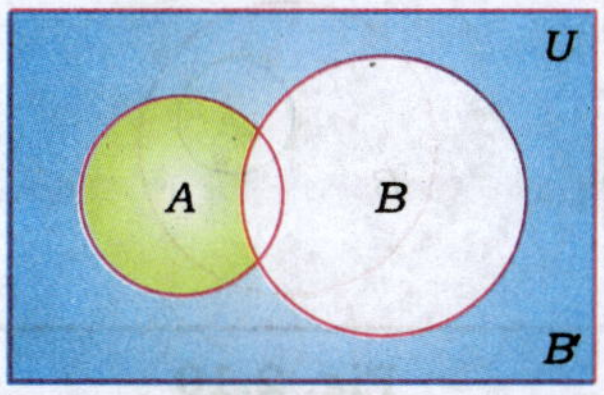

Fig. 2.4

8. In the Fig. (2.5), shaded portion represents $(A \cap B)'$.

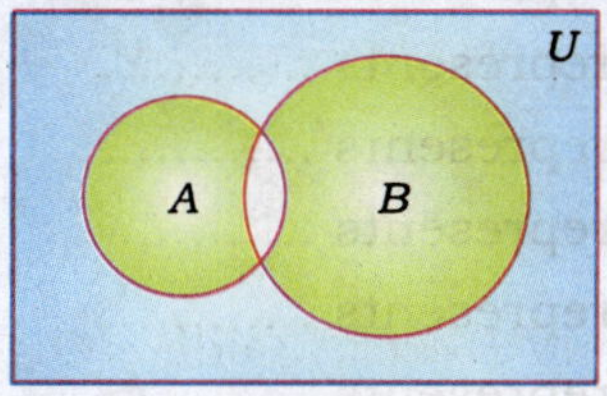

Fig. 2.5

9. In the Fig. (2.6), shaded portion represents $(A \cup B)'$

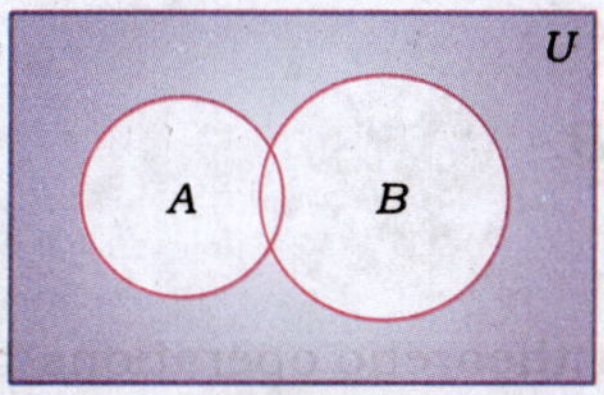

Fig. 2.6

10. In the Fig. (2.7), shaded portion represents $A' \cap B$ which is similar as $B - A$.

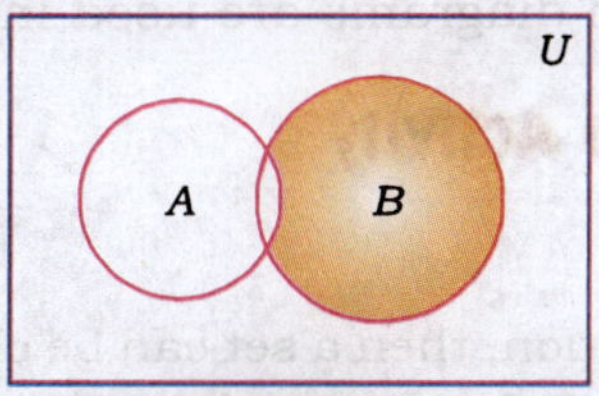

Fig. 2.7

11. In the Fig. (2.8), shaded portion represents $A' \cup B$.

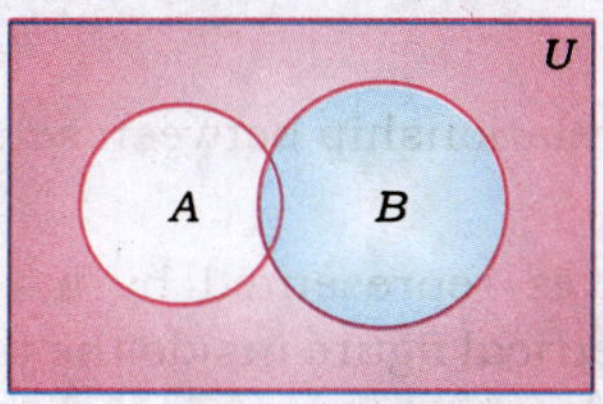

Fig. 2.8

12. Fig. (2.9) shows $A \cap B = \phi$.

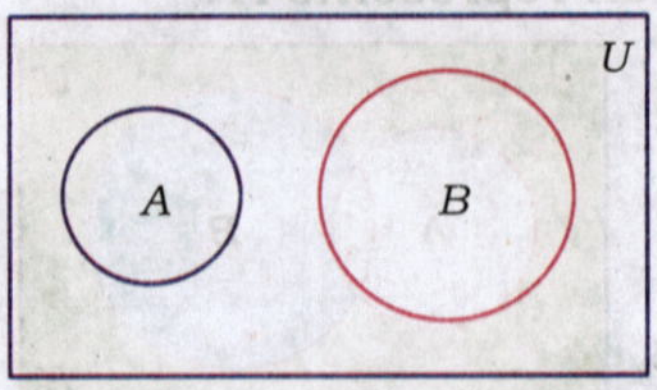

Fig. 2.9

13. Fig. (2.10) shows $A \subset B$.

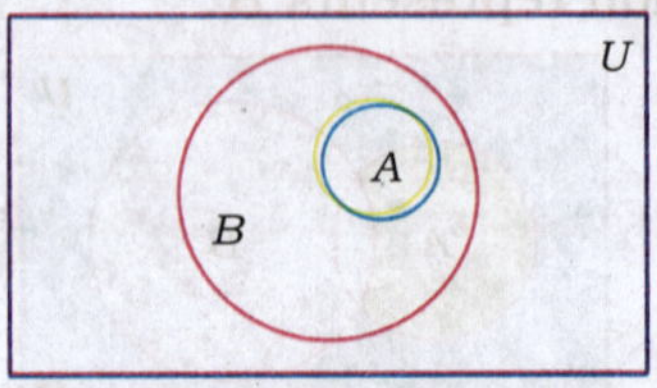

Fig. 2.10

Observation

1. Coloured portion in Fig. (2.1) represents ....
2. Coloured portion in Fig. (2.2) represents ....
3. Coloured portion in Fig. (2.3) represents ....
4. Coloured portion in Fig. (2.4) represents ....
5. Coloured portion in Fig. (2.5) represents ....
6. Coloured portion in Fig. (2.6) represents ....
7. Coloured portion in Fig. (2.7) represents ....
8. Coloured portion in Fig. (2.8) represents ....
9. Fig. (2.9) shows that $(A \cap B) =$ ....
10. Fig. (2.10) represent A .... B.

Result

We have learnt how to represent set theoretic operations by using Venn diagrams.

Application

Set theoretic representation of Venn diagrams are used in Logic and Mathematics.

Necessary Concepts Related to Activity

1. Universal Set

If there are some sets under consideration, then a set can be chosen arbitrarily which is a superset of each one of the given sets. Such a set is known as the universal set and it is denoted by U.
e.g. Let $A = \{2, 4, 6\}$, $B = \{1, 3, 5\}$ and $C = \{0, 7\}$. Then, $U = \{0, 1, 2, 3, 4, 5, 6, 7\}$ is an universal set.

2. Venn Diagrams

Venn diagrams represent most of the relationship between sets. These diagrams consist of rectangles and closed curves usually circles.

In Venn diagrams, the universal set is represented by a rectangular region and its subset are represented by circle or a closed geometrical figure inside the universal set. Also, an element of a set is represented by a point within the circle of set.

e.g. If $U = \{1, 2, 3, 4, \ldots, 10\}$ and $A = \{1, 2, 3\}$, then its Venn diagram is as shown in the Figure (2.11).

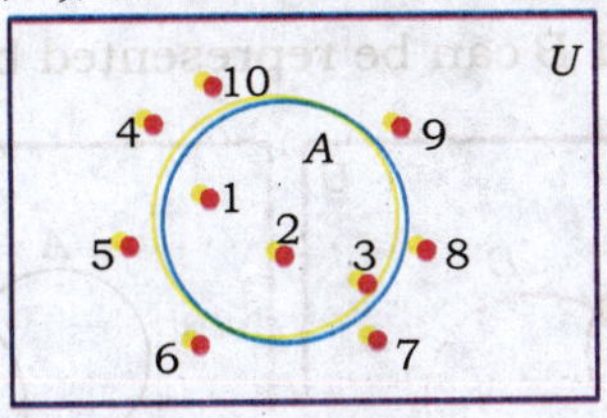

Fig. 2.11

3. Operations on Sets

(i) **Union of Sets** Let A and B be any two sets. The union of A and B is the set of all those elements which belong to either in A or in B (including those which are not in both). It is denoted by $A \cup B$ and read as ***A*** union ***B.*** The symbol '$\cup$' is used to denote the union.

$\therefore \quad A \cup B = \{x : x \in A \text{ or } x \in B\}$

e.g. Let $A = \{2, 3\}$ and $B = \{3, 4, 5\}$.

Then, $\quad A \cup B = \{2, 3, 4, 5\}$

The union of sets A and B is represented by the following Venn diagram

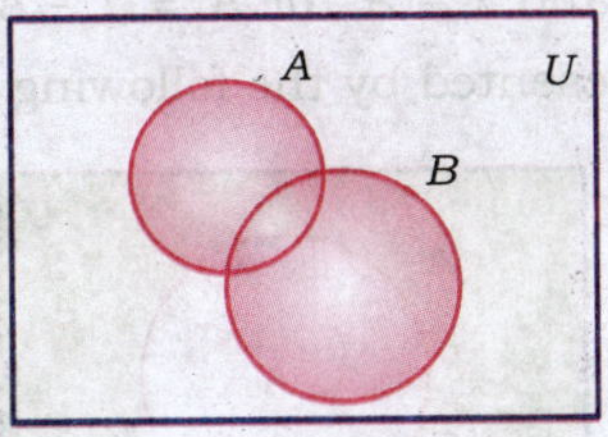

Fig. 2.12

The shaded portion represents $A \cup B$.

(ii) **Intersection of Sets** Let A and B be any two sets. The intersection of A and B is the set of all those elements which belong to both A and B. It is denoted by $A \cap B$ and read as ***A* intersection *B***. The symbol '$\cap$' is used to denote the intersection.

$\therefore \quad A \cap B = \{x : x \in A \text{ and } x \in B\}$

The intersection of sets A and B is represented by the following Venn diagram

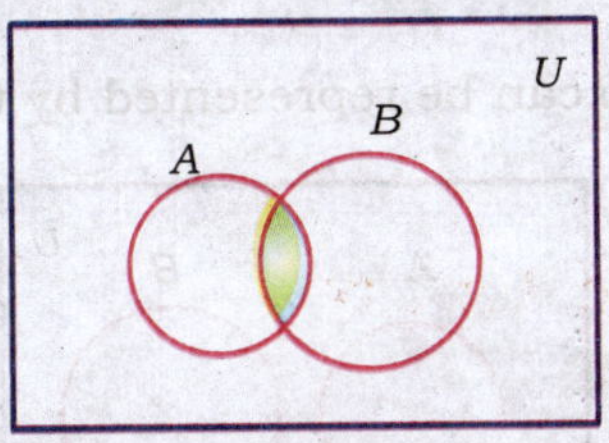

Fig. 2.13

The shaded portion represents $A \cap B$.

e.g. Let $A = \{2, 3, 4, 5\}$ and $B = \{1, 3, 6, 4\}$.

Then, $A \cap B = \{3, 4\}$

(iii) **Difference of Sets** Let A and B be any two sets. The difference of sets A and B in this order is the set of all those elements of A which do not belong to B. It is denoted by $\boldsymbol{A - B}$ and read as ***A* minus *B***.

The symbol '**–**' is used to denote the difference of sets.

$\therefore \quad A - B = \{x : x \in A \text{ and } x \notin B\}$

Similarly, $B - A = \{x : x \in B \text{ and } x \notin A\}$

The difference of two sets A and B can be represented by the following Venn diagram

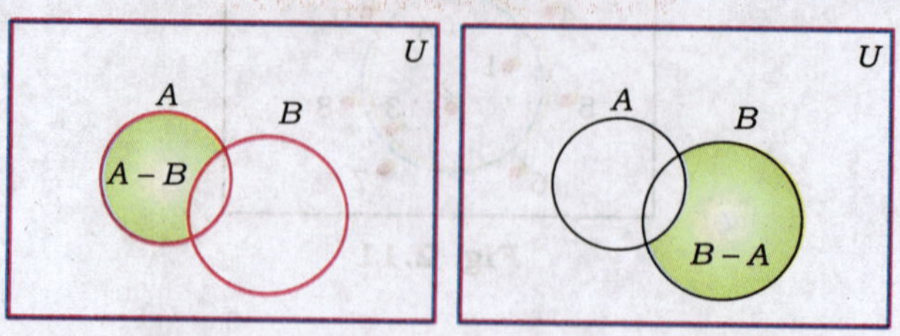

Fig. 2.14

The shaded portion represents the difference of two sets A and B.

e.g. Let $A = \{1, 2, 3, 4, 5\}$ and $B = \{3, 5, 7, 9\}$.

Then, $A - B = \{1, 2, 4\}$ and $B - A = \{7, 9\}$

(iv) **Complement of a Set** Let U be the universal set and A be any subset of set U, then complement of A with respect to U is the set of all those elements of U which are not in A. It is denoted by $\overline{A}$ or A' and read as, **'*A* complement'**.

Thus, $\overline{A} = \{x : x \in U \text{ and } x \notin A\}$ or $A' = U - A$

The complement of set A is represented by the following Venn diagram

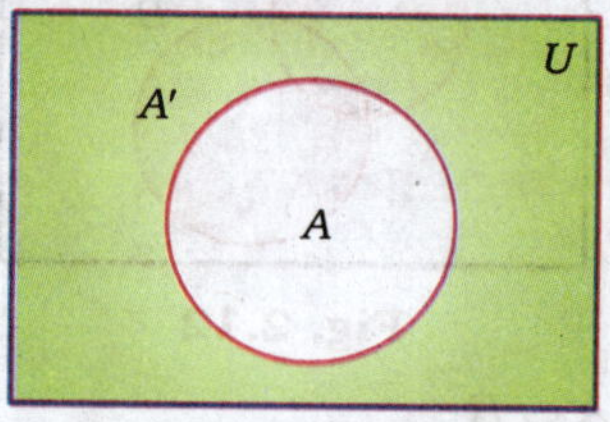

Fig. 2.15

Here, the shaded portion represents the complement of set A.

e.g. Let $U = \{1, 2, 3, 4, 5, 6\}$ and $A = \{2, 4\}$.

Then, $A' = U - A = \{1, 2, 3, 4, 5, 6\} - \{2, 4\} = \{1, 3, 5, 6\}$

(v) **Disjoint Sets** Two sets A and B are said to be disjoint sets, if thcy have **no common element** i.e. $A \cap B = \phi$.

The disjoint of two sets A and B can be represented by the Venn diagram.

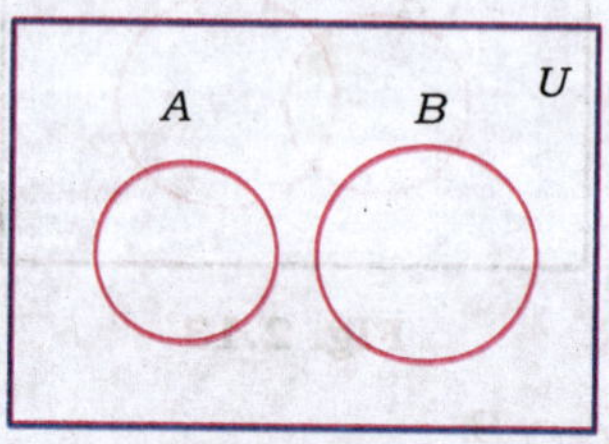

Fig. 2.16

e.g. Let $A = \{2, 4, 6\}$ and $B = \{1, 3, 5\}$

Then, $A \cap B = \phi$. Hence, A and B are disjoint sets.

Viva-Voce

Q.1 Explain about the 'Union of sets'.

Ans The union of sets A and B is the set of all those elements which belongs to either A or B or to both.

Q.2 If A and B are two disjoint sets, then $n(A \cup B)$ is equal to ....

Ans $n(A) + n(B)$

Q.3 'If A is a subset of the universal set U, then its complement A' is also a subset of U.' Is it true or false?

Ans True.

Q.4 If A and B are two sets having 4 and 7 elements, respectively, then write the maximum number of elements that $A \cup B$ can have.

Ans 11

Q.5 Explain about the 'disjoint sets'.

Ans Two sets A and B are said to be disjoint, if $A \cap B = \phi$.

Q.6 $(A \cup B)' = U - (A \cup B)$. Is it true or false?

Ans True

Q.7 If A be any set, then $A \cup A' =$ ....

Ans U (universal set).

Q.8 Write the De-Morgan's law for any two sets A and B.

Ans (i) $(A \cup B)' = A' \cap B'$ (ii) $(A \cap B)' = A' \cup B'$

Q.9 Write the complement of universal set.

Ans ϕ

Activity 3

OBJECTIVE

To verify distributive law for three given non-empty sets A, B and C, that is, $A \cup (B \cap C) = (A \cup B) \cap (A \cup C)$.

Material Required

Cardboard, white thick sheets of paper, different coloured pencils, scissors, gum.

Prerequisite Knowledge

1. Concept of universal set.
2. Concept of union of sets.
3. Concept of intersection of sets.
4. Distributive law.

Method of Construction

1. Firstly, cut five rectangular strips from a white sheet of paper and paste them on the cardboard in such a way that three of the rectangles are in horizontal line and two of the remaining rectangles are also placed horizontally in a line just below the above three rectangles. Write the symbol U in the left/right top corner of each rectangle as shown in Fig. (3.1) to Fig. (3.5).
2. Drawn three circles and mark them as A, B and C in each of the five rectangles as shown in the below figures.
3. Colour/shade the portions as shown in the figures.

Demonstration

1. Here, U denotes the universal set represented by the rectangle in each figure.
2. Subsets of the universal set U are represented by circles A, B and C.

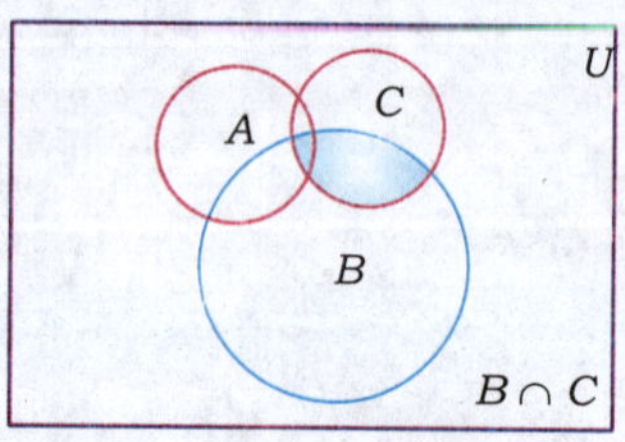

Fig. 3.1

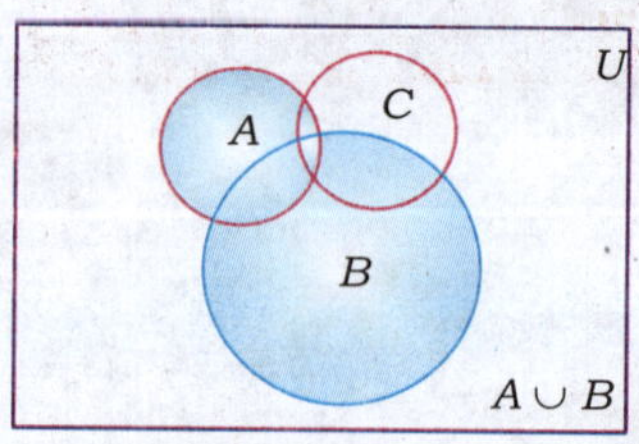

Fig. 3.2

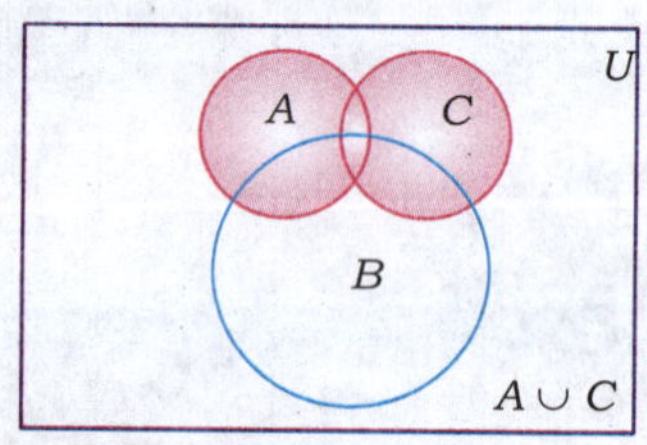

Fig. 3.3

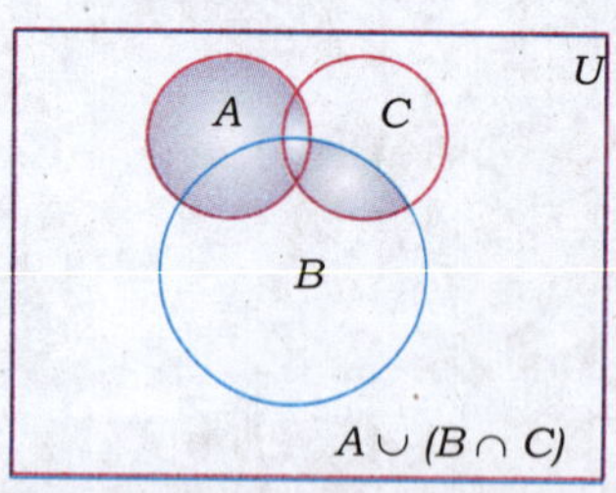

Fig. 3.4

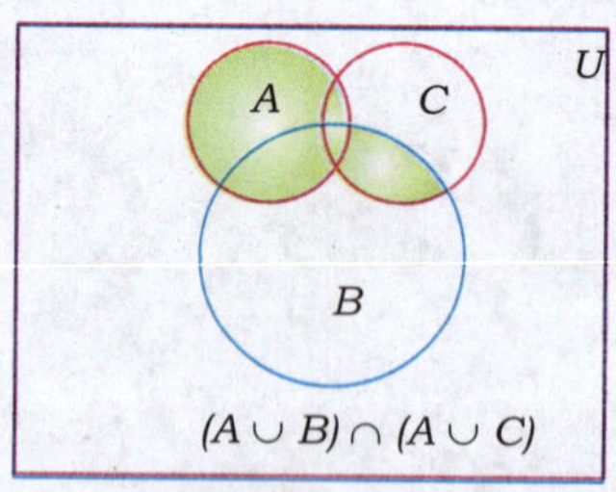

Fig. 3.5

3. In Fig. 3.1 shaded portion represents $B \cap C$, shaded portions in Fig. 3.2 represents $A \cup B$, Fig. 3.3 represents $A \cup C$, Fig. 3.4 represents $A \cup (B \cap C)$ and shaded portion in Fig. 3.5 represents $(A \cup B) \cap (A \cup C)$.

Observation

1. Coloured portion in Fig. (3.1) represents ....
2. Coloured portion in Fig. (3.2) represents ....
3. Coloured portion in Fig. (3.3) represents ....
4. Coloured portion in Fig. (3.4) represents ....
5. Coloured portion in Fig. (3.5) represents ....
6. The common shaded portions in Fig. (3.4) and Fig. (3.5) are ....
7. $A \cup (B \cap C) =$ ....

The coloured portion in Fig. (3.4) and Fig. (3.5) are the same.

Hence, the distributive law is verified.

In the same way, the other distributive law $A \cap (B \cup C) = (A \cap B) \cup (A \cap C)$ can also be verified.

Result

We have learnt distributive law for three given non-empty sets and how to verify it.

Application

Distributivity property of set operations is used in the simplification of problems involving set operations.

Necessary Concepts Related to Activity

1. **Concept of universal set** Refer to Activity 2.
2. **Concept of union of sets** Refer to Activity 2.
3. **Concept of intersection of sets** Refer to Activity 2.
4. **Distributive Law** If A, B and C are any three sets, then
   (i) $A \cap (B \cup C) = (A \cap B) \cup (A \cap C)$ i.e. intersection distributes over union.
   (ii) $A \cup (B \cap C) = (A \cup B) \cap (A \cup C)$ i.e. union distributes over intersection.

Viva-Voce

Q.1 **If A and B are two sets, then $(A \cup B) \cap (A \cup B')$ is equal to ....**

Ans A

Q.2 **If A and B be two sets such that $B \subset A$, then $(A - B) \cup B =$ ....**

Ans A

Q.3 **If $A \cap B' = \phi$, then $B \subseteq A$. Is it true or false?**

Ans False

Q.4 **For any two sets A and B described as $A \cup (A \cap B) = A$, is it true?**

Ans Yes, it is true.

Q.5 **In which law of sets the property $(A \cap B) \cap C = A \cap (B \cap C)$ satisfies?**

Ans Associative law.

Q.6 **'If A, B and C are any three sets, then $A \cup (B \cap C) = (A \cup B) \cap (A \cup C)$ also known as union distributes over intersection'. Is it true or false?**

Ans True

Q.7 **The name of law which is applied in $A \cap \phi = \phi$ is ....**

Ans Identity law

Q.8 **Apply distributive law on $A \cap (A \cup B)$, do we get a simplified form?**

Ans A

Q.9 **If $A \cap (B \cup C) = (A \cap B) \cup (A \cap C)$. Is it true or false?**

Ans True

Q.10 **If $A \cap (B - C) = (A \cap B) - (A \cup C)$. Is it true or false?**

Ans False

Activity 4

OBJECTIVE

To identify a relation and a function.

Material Required

Cardboard, battery, electric bulbs of two different colours, testing screws, tester, electrical wires and switches.

Prerequisite Knowledge

1. Concept of ordered pair.
2. Concept of relation.
3. Concept of function.

Methods of Construction

1. Firstly, take a piece of cardboard of suitable size and paste a white paper on it.
2. Drill eight holes on the left side of board in a column and mark them as A, B, C, D, E, F, G and H as shown in the Fig. (4.1).

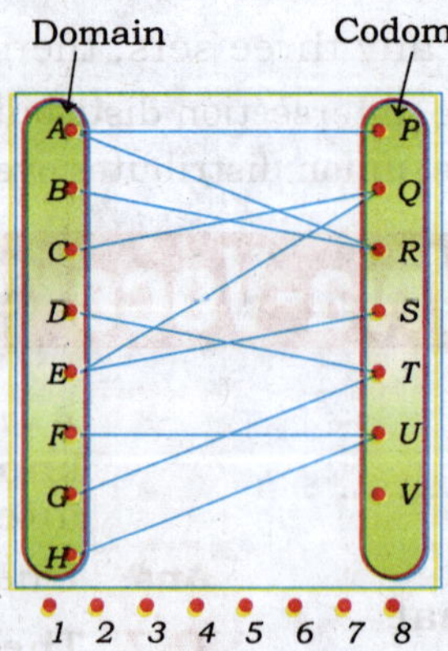

Fig. 4.1

3. Drill seven holes on the right side of the board in a column and mark them as P, Q, R, S, T, U and V as shown in the Fig (4.1).
4. After that, fix bulbs of same colour in the holes A, B, C, D, E, F, G and H.
5. Similarly, fix bulbs of the other colour in the holes P, Q, R, S, T, U and V.
6. In the bottom of the board fix testing screws marked as 1, 2, 3, ..., 8.
7. Complete the electrical circuits in such a manner that a pair of corresponding bulbs, one from each column glow simultaneously.
8. These pairs of bulbs will give ordered pairs, which will constitute a relation which in turn may/may not be a function [see Fig. (4.1)].

Demonstration

1. Bulbs at $A, B, ..., H$, along the left column represent domain and bulbs along the right column at $P, Q, R, ..., V$ represent codomain.
2. We can obtain different order pairs out of given eight screws by using two or more testing screws. In Fig. (4.1), all the eight screws have been used to give different ordered pairs such as (A, P), (B, R), (C, Q), (A, R), (E, Q), etc.
3. By choosing different ordered pairs make different sets of ordered pairs.

Observation

1. In Fig. (4.1), ordered pairs are ....
2. These ordered pairs constitute a ....
3. The ordered pairs (A, P), (B, R), (C, Q), (E, Q), (D, T), (G, T), (F, U), (H, U) constitute a relation which is also a ....
4. The ordered pairs (B, R), (C, Q), (D, T), (E, S), (E, Q) constitute a .... which is not a ....

Result

We have learnt how to identify a relation and a function.

Application

The activity can be used to explain the concept of a relation and a function. It can also be used to explain the concept of one-one, onto functions.

Necessary Concepts Related to Activity

1. Ordered Pairs

If a pair of elements written in circular bracket and grouped together in a particular order, then such a pair, is called an ordered pair. Ordered pair is written by listing two objects in the specific order, separated by comma (,) and enclosing the pair in parentheses.

e.g. The ordered pair of two elements a and b is denoted by (a, b) ; a is first element (or first component) and b is second element (or second component).

Two ordered pairs are equal if their corresponding elements are equal

i.e. $(a, b) = (c, d) \Rightarrow a = c$ and $b = d$

2. Relation

Let A and B be two non-empty sets. Then, a relation R from set A to set B is a subset of cartesian product $A \times B$ i.e. $R \subseteq A \times B$.

The subset is derived by describing a relationship between the first element and the second element of the ordered pairs in $A \times B$. The second element is called **image** of first element.

If $(a, b) \in R$, then we write it as aRb and we say that **a is related to b by the relation R**.

If $(a, b) \notin R$, then we write it as $a \not{R} b$ and we say that **a is not related to b by the relation R**.

3. Function as a Relation

A relation f from a non-empty set A to a non-empty set B is said to be a function, if every element of set A has one and only one image in set B.

If f is a function from a set A to a set B, then we write

$$f : A \to B \text{ or } A \xrightarrow{f} B$$

and it is read as f is a function from A to B or f maps A to B.

If $(a, b) \in f \Rightarrow f(a) = b$.

Here, b is called the image of a under f and a is called the pre-image of b under f.

Viva-Voce

Q.1 Describe about the ordered pair.

Ans An ordered pair consists of two objects or elements in a particular order.

Q.2 In how many forms relation can be represented?

Ans Generally, relation is defined in three forms as following

(i) Roster form (ii) Set builder form

(iii) Arrow diagram

Q.3 $f : A \to B$ is a function, if an element in A does not have an image in B. Is it true or false?

Ans False

Q.4 Write the relation $R = \{(x, x^3) : x$ is a prime number less than $10\}$ in Roster form.

Ans $R = \{(2, 8), (3, 27), (5, 125), (7, 343)\}$

Q.5 If $A = \{1, 2, 3, 4\}$ and $B = \{5, 6, 7, 8\}$, then identify which of the following are relations from A to B?

(i) $R_1 = \{(1, 5), (2, 7), (3, 8)\}$

(ii) $R_2 = \{(6, 2), (3, 7), (4, 7)\}$

Ans (i) Since, $R_1 \subseteq A \times B$, therefore R_1 is a relation from set A to B.

(ii) Since, $(6, 2) \in R_2$ but $(6, 2) \notin A \times B$, i.e. $R_2 \nsubseteq A \times B$, therefore R_2 is not a relation from A to B.

Q.6 'A function 'f' from a non-empty set A to a non-empty set B, associate each element of set A to a unique element of set B.' Is it true or false?

Ans True

Q.7 Identify the relation $\{(2, 0), (4, 8), (2, 1), (3, 6)\}$ is function or not.

Ans It is not a function, because first element 2 corresponds to two different images 0 and 1.

Q.8 If $(3a - 2, b + 3) = (2a - 1, 3)$, then values of a and b are.

Ans Since, $(3a - 2, b + 3) = (2a - 1, 3)$ then by equality of ordered pairs,

$$3a - 2 = 2a - 1$$

$\Rightarrow \quad a = 1$ and $b + 3 = 3 \Rightarrow b = 0$

Activity 5

OBJECTIVE

To distinguish between a relation and a function.

Material Required

Cardboard, drawing sheets of different colours, scissors, gum, strings or wire, nails etc.

Prerequisite Knowledge

1. Concept of ordered pair.
2. Concept of relation.
3. Concept of function.

Method of Construction

1. Take a piece of cardboard of convenient size and fix a coloured sheet on it.
2. Take a different colour drawing sheet and cut out a rectangular strip of size 4 cm × 3 cm and paste it on the left side of the drawing board. (see Fig. (5.1))
3. Fix three nails on this strip and mark them as *a, b, c.* (see Fig. (5.1))
4. Cut out another colour rectangular strip of size 4 cm × 3 cm and paste it on the right hand side of the drawing board. (see Fig. (5.2))
5. Fix two nails on the right side of this strip (see Fig. (5.2)) and mark them as 1 and 2.

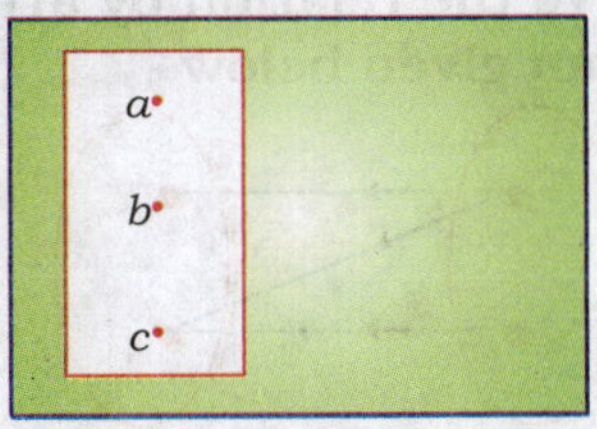

Fig. 5.1

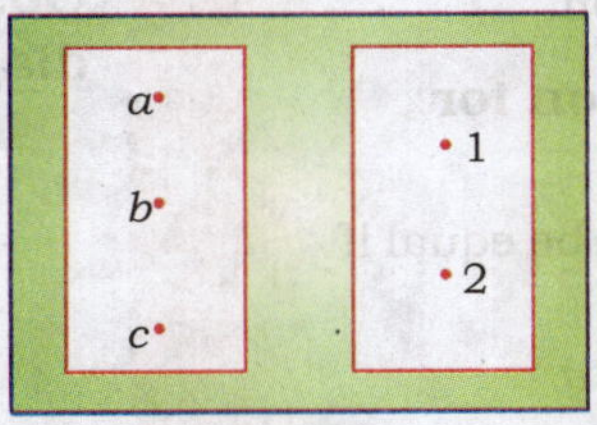

Fig. 5.2

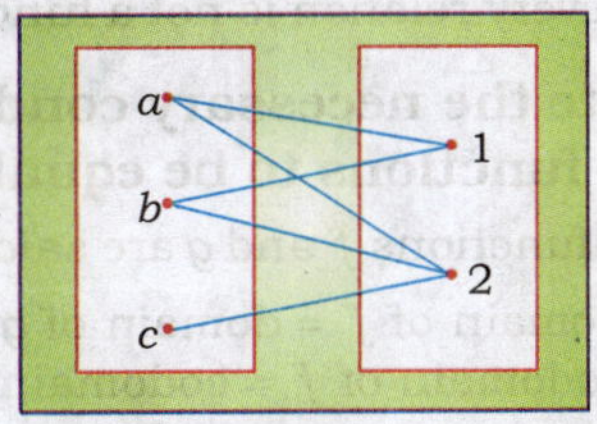

Fig. 5.3

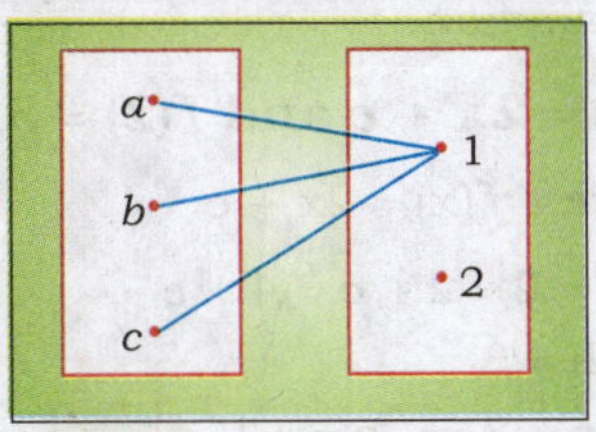

Fig. 5.4

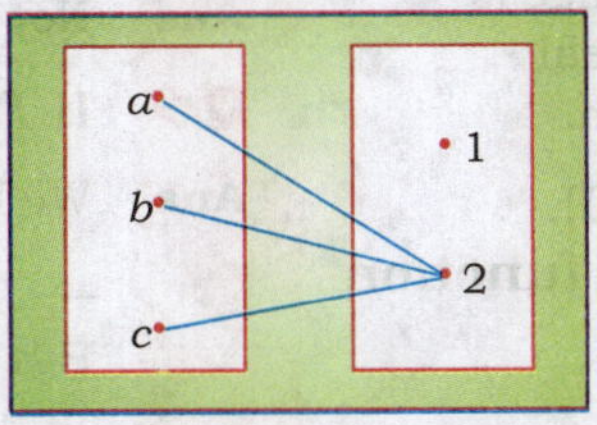

Fig. 5.5

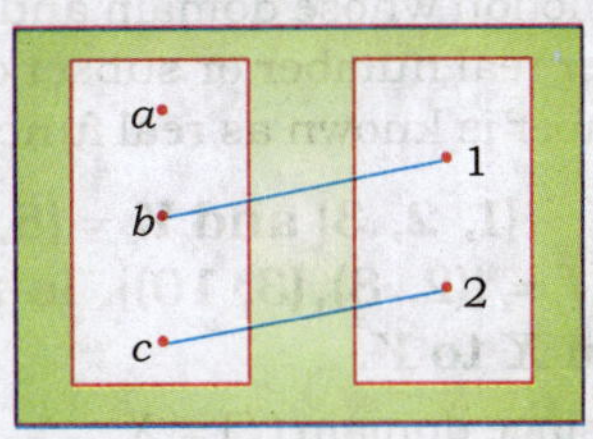

Fig. 5.6

Demonstration

1. Join nails of the left hand strip to the nails on the right hand strip by strings or wires in different ways as per your choice. Some of such ways are shown in Fig. (5.3) to Fig. (5.6).
2. Joining nails in each figure constitute different ordered pairs, which represent elements of a relation.

Observation

1. In Fig. (5.3), ordered pairs are .... These ordered pairs constitute a .... but not a ....
2. In Fig. (5.4), ordered pairs are .... These constitute a .... as well as ....
3. In Fig. (5.5), ordered pairs are .... These ordered pairs constitute a .... as well as ....
4. In Fig. (5.6), ordered pairs are .... These ordered pairs do not represent .... but represent ....

Result

We have learnt how to distinguish between a relation and a function.

Application

This activity can also be used to understand different type of functions such as constant function, identity function, injective and surjective functions, by joining nails on the left hand strip to that of right hand strip in different manner. We can also change the number of nails on both the sides to describe different types of relations and functions.

Necessary Concepts Related to Activity

1. **Ordered pair** Refer to Activity 4. 2. **Relation** Refer to Activity 4. 3. **Function** Refer to Activity 4.

Viva-Voce

Q.1 Is every function a relation?

Ans Yes, every function is relation.

Q.2 Is every relation a function?

Ans No, every relation is not a function.

Q.3 Write the necessary condition for two functions to be equal.

Ans Two functions f and g are said to be equal if

(i) domain of f = domain of g

(ii) codomain of f = codomain of g

Q.4 Define a real function.

Ans A function whose domain and range is either real number or subset of real number is known as real function.

Q.5 If $X = \{1, 2, 3\}$ and $Y = \{8, 10\}$. Let $f = \{(2, 8), (3, 10)\}$. Is f a function from X to Y.

Ans No, since domain $(f) \neq X$.

Q.6 Which of the relations are function?

(i) $f_1 = \{(2, 1), (3, 1), (4, 1), (3, 2), (4, 2), (4, 3)\}$

(ii) $f_2 = \{(1, 4), (2, 3), (3, 2), (4, 1)\}$

Ans f_1 is not a function but f_2 is a function.

Q.7 $f : A \to B$ is not a function, if there is an element in A which has more than one image in B. Is it true or false?

Ans True

Q.8 Observe the relation by arrow diagram given below

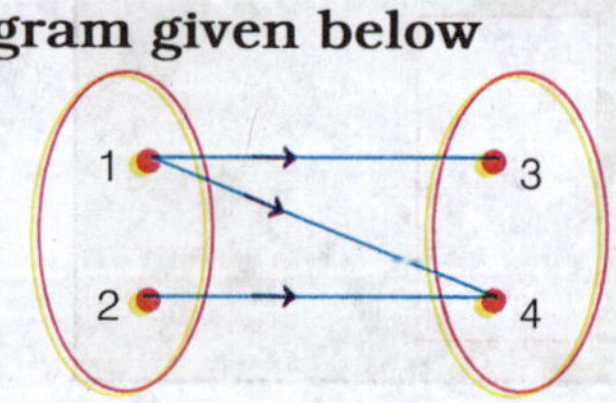

and say is it function or not?

Ans Not a function.

Q.9 If $f(x) = 2x + c$ and $f(2) = 3$, find c.

Ans We have, $f(x) = 2x + c$

$\Rightarrow f(2) = 2 \times 2 + c = 4 + c$

But $f(2) = 3$

$\therefore \quad 4 + c = 3 \Rightarrow \quad c = -1$

Q.10 Let $f : R \to R$ is given by $f(x) = x^2 + 3$. Find $\{x : f(x) = 28\}$

Ans Given, $f(x) = x^2 + 3$ and $f(x) = 28$

$\therefore \quad x^2 + 3 = 28$

$\Rightarrow \quad x^2 = 25 \Rightarrow x = \pm 5$

$\therefore \quad x \in \{-5, 5\}$

Activity 6

OBJECTIVE

To verify the relation between the degree measure and the radian measure of an angle.

Material Required

Bangle, geometry box, thread or string, marker, cardboard, gum, white sheet paper.

Prerequisite Knowledge

1. Concept of degree measure.
2. Concept of radian measure.

Method of Construction

1. Take a cardboard of a convenient size and fix a white paper on it.
2. On white paper draw a circle using a bangle.
3. Place set square at two different positions and find diameters PQ and RS of the circle (see Fig. 6.1 and Fig. 6.2).

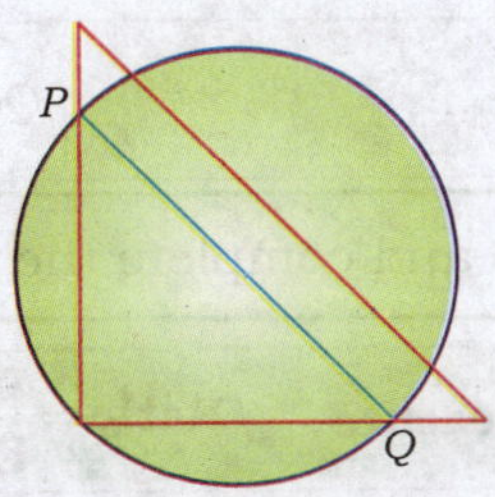

Fig. 6.1

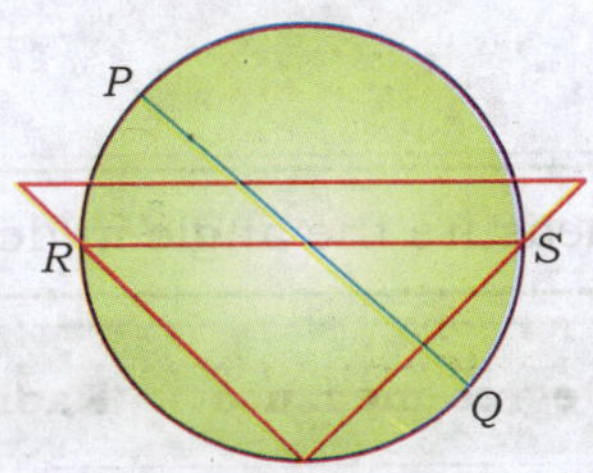

Fig. 6.2

4. Denote the point as C, where PQ and RS intersect. Thus, the point C will be the centre of the circle (Fig. 6.3).

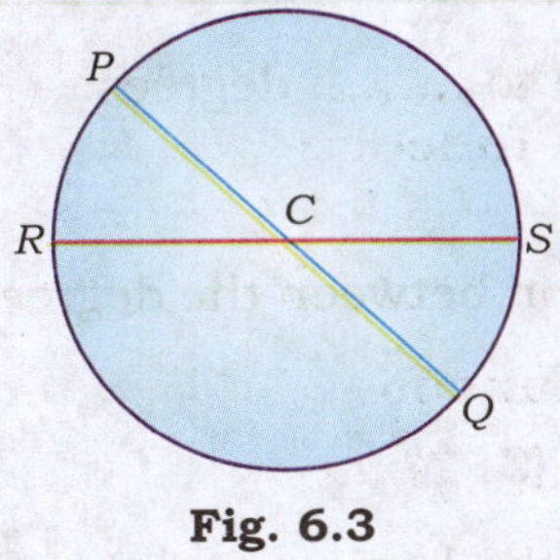

Fig. 6.3

5. Hence, $CP = CR = CS = CQ =$ radius.

Demonstration

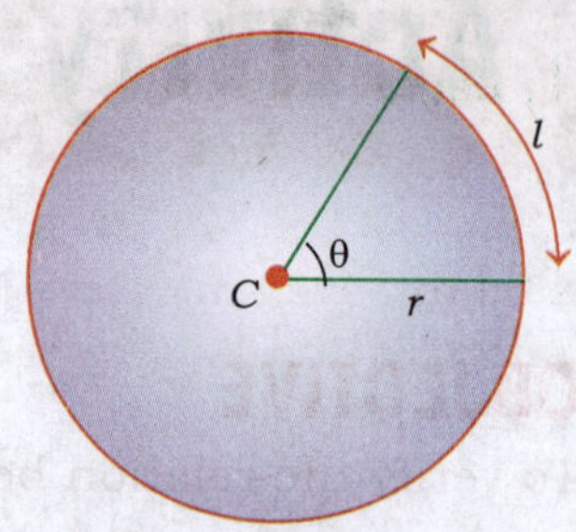

Fig. 6.4

1. Let the radius of the circle be r and l be the length of an arc subtending an angle θ at the centre of the circle (Fig. 6.4). $\theta = \frac{l}{r}$ radians.
2. Let degree measure of $\theta = \frac{l}{2\pi r} \times 360$ degrees.

   Then, $\frac{l}{r}$ radians $= \frac{l}{2\pi r} \times 360$ degrees.

   $\therefore$ 1 radian $= \left(\frac{180}{\pi}\right)^{\circ} = (57.27)^{\circ}$

Observation

1. Using thread or string, measure arc lengths RP, PS, SQ, QR and record them in the table given below

S.No.	Arc	Length of arc (l)	Radius of circle (r)	Radian measure
1.	$\overset{\frown}{RP}$	......	......	$\angle RCP = \frac{\overset{\frown}{RP}}{r} =$ ......
2.	$\overset{\frown}{PS}$	......	......	$\angle PCS = \frac{\overset{\frown}{PS}}{r} =$ ......
3.	$\overset{\frown}{SQ}$	......	......	$\angle SCQ = \frac{\overset{\frown}{SQ}}{r} =$ ......
4.	$\overset{\frown}{QR}$	......	......	$\angle QCR = \frac{\overset{\frown}{QR}}{r} =$ ......

2. Using protractor, measure the angle in degrees and complete the table.

Angle	Degree measure	Radian measure	Ratio $= \frac{\text{Degree measure}}{\text{Radian measure}}$
$\angle RCP$	....	....	....
$\angle PCS$	....	....	....
$\angle QCS$	....	....	....
$\angle QCR$	....	....	....

3. The value of one radian is equal to .... degrees.

Result

We have learnt how to verify the relation between the degree measure and the radian measure of an angle.

Application

This activity is useful in the study of the basic concepts of angle and trigonometric functions.

Necessary Concepts Related to Activity

1. Degree Measure (Sexagesimal System)

If the rotation from initial side to terminal side is $\left(\frac{1}{360}\right)$th of a complete revolution, then the angle is said to have a measure of one degree (1°). One degree is divided into 60 equal parts, called **minutes** and 1 minute is denoted by 1′. One minute is divided into 60 equal parts, called **second** and 1 second is denoted by 1″.

Thus, $1° = 60'$; $1' = 60''$

2. Radian Measure (Circular System)

Angle subtended at the centre by an arc of length one unit in a circle of radius 1 unit is said to have a measure of 1 radian.

In general, in a circle of radius r having an arc of length r will subtend an angle of 1 radian at the centre. 1 radian is written as 1^c.

Also, a circle of radius r having an arc of length l will subtend an angle θ radian at the centre, where

$$\theta = \frac{l}{r} = \frac{\text{Length of arc}}{\text{Radius}} \text{ or } l = r\,\theta$$

The figures below show the angles, whose measures are 1 radian (1^c) and –1 radian (-1^c).

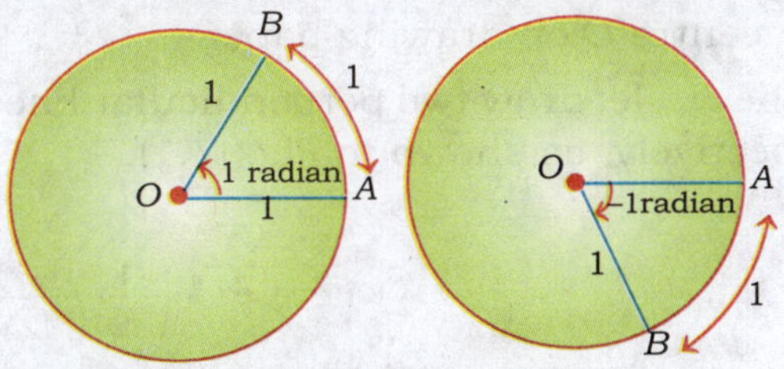

Fig. 6.5

Relation between Degree and Radian

- Radian measure $= \frac{\pi}{180°} \times$ Degree measure
- Degree measure $= \frac{180°}{\pi} \times$ Radian measure

Viva-Voce

Q.1 Define measure of an angle.

Ans The amount of rotation from the initial side to the terminal side, is called the measure of an angle.

Q.2 Radian measure $= \frac{\pi}{180°} \times$ Degree measure. Is it true or false?

Ans True

Q.3 In circular measure system, the angle is measured in ....

Ans Radians.

Q.4 Write the relation between degree and radian.

Ans 2π radian = 360°; π radian = 180°

$1 \text{ radian} = \frac{180°}{\pi}$

Q.5 Define 1 radian.

Ans Angle subtended at the centre by an arc of length one unit in a circle of radius 1 unit is said to have a measure of 1 radian.

Q.6 Convert 240° into radian.

Ans $240° = \frac{\pi}{180°} \times 240° \text{ radian} = \frac{4\pi}{3} \text{ radian.}$

Q.7 Convert $\frac{\pi}{8}$ radian into degree.

Ans $\frac{\pi}{8} \text{ radian} = \left(\frac{\pi}{8} \times \frac{180}{\pi}\right)^\circ = \left(\frac{180}{8}\right)^\circ$

$= \left(\frac{45}{2}\right)^\circ = 22\frac{1}{2}^\circ = 22°30'$

Activity 7

OBJECTIVE

To find the values of sine and cosine functions in second, third and fourth quadrants using their given values in first quadrant.

Material Required

Drawing board, drawing sheet, different coloured pens, glue, wires and needle etc.

Prerequisite Knowledge

Concept of sign of trigonometric function in different quadrants.

Method of Construction

1. Take a drawing board of suitable size and fix a drawing sheet with glue on it.
2. Draw a unit circle with centre O on drawing paper.
3. Through the centre of the circle, draw two perpendicular lines $X'OX$ and YOY' representing X-axis and Y-axis, respectively, as shown in Fig. (7.1).

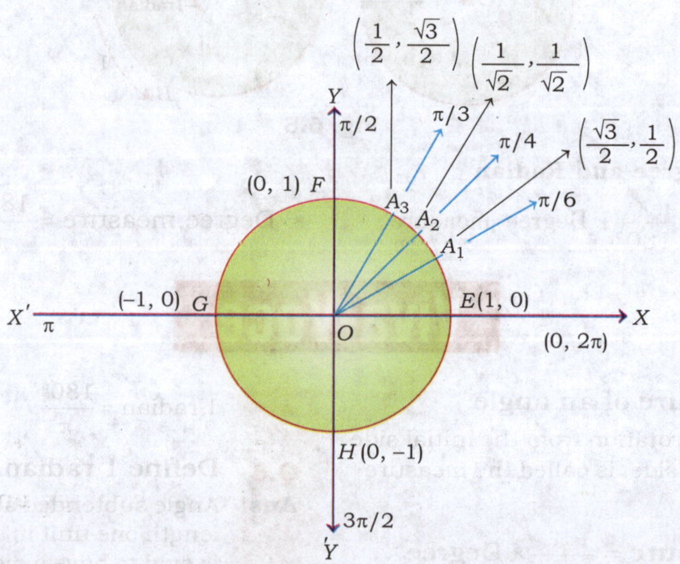

Fig. 7.1

4. Mark the points as E, F, G and H, where the circle cuts the X-axis and Y-axis, respectively, as shown in Fig. (7.1).
5. Through O, draw angles A_1OX, A_2OX and A_3OX of measures $\frac{\pi}{6}$, $\frac{\pi}{4}$ and $\frac{\pi}{3}$, respectively.
6. Take a needle of unit length. Fix one end of it at the centre of the circle and the other end to move freely along the circle.

Demonstration

1. The coordinates of the point A_1 are $\left(\frac{\sqrt{3}}{2}, \frac{1}{2}\right)$ because its x-coordinate is $\cos\frac{\pi}{6}$ and y-coordinate is $\sin\frac{\pi}{6}$. The coordinates of the points A_2 and A_3 are $\left(\frac{1}{\sqrt{2}}, \frac{1}{\sqrt{2}}\right)$ and $\left(\frac{1}{2}, \frac{\sqrt{3}}{2}\right)$, respectively.
2. To find the value of sine or cosine of some angle in the second quadrant (say) $\frac{2\pi}{3}$, rotate the needle in anti-clockwise direction making an angle at A_4OX of measure $\frac{2\pi}{3}$ = 120° with the positive direction of X-axis.

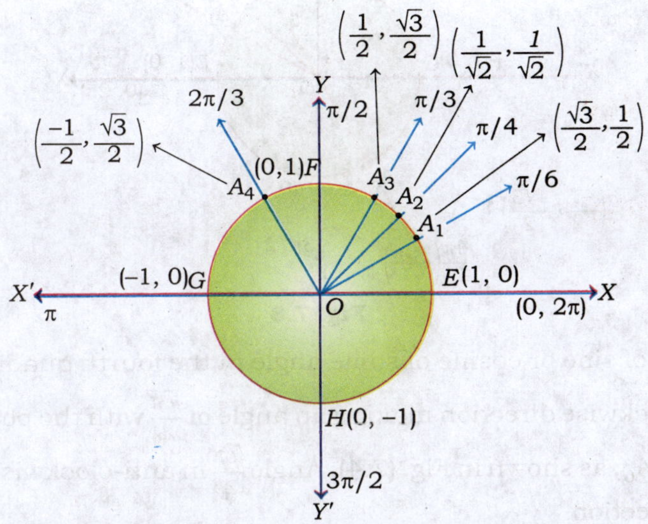

Fig. 7.2

3. Look at the position OA_4 of the needle in Fig. (7.2). Since, $\frac{2\pi}{3} = \pi - \frac{\pi}{3}$, OA_4 is the mirror image of OA_3 with respect to Y-axis. Therefore, the coordinate of A_4 are $\left(-\frac{1}{2}, \frac{\sqrt{3}}{2}\right)$. Thus, $\sin\frac{2\pi}{3} = \frac{\sqrt{3}}{2}$ and $\cos\frac{2\pi}{3} = -\frac{1}{2}$.
4. To find the value of sine or cosine of some angle say, $\pi + \frac{\pi}{3} = \frac{4\pi}{3}$, i.e. $\frac{-2\pi}{3}$ (say) in the third quadrant, rotate the needle in anti-clockwise direction making an angle of $\frac{4\pi}{3}$ with the positive direction of X-axis.

5. Look at the new position OA_5 of the needle, which is shown in Fig. (7.3). Point A_5 is the mirror image of the point A_4 (since, $\angle A_4OX = A_5OX$) with respect to X-axis. Therefore, coordinates of A_5 are $\left(-\frac{1}{2}, \frac{-\sqrt{3}}{2}\right)$ and hence, $\sin\left(-\frac{2\pi}{3}\right) = \sin\left(\frac{4\pi}{3}\right) = -\frac{\sqrt{3}}{2}$ and $\cos\left(-\frac{2\pi}{3}\right) = \cos\left(\frac{4\pi}{3}\right) = -\frac{1}{2}$.

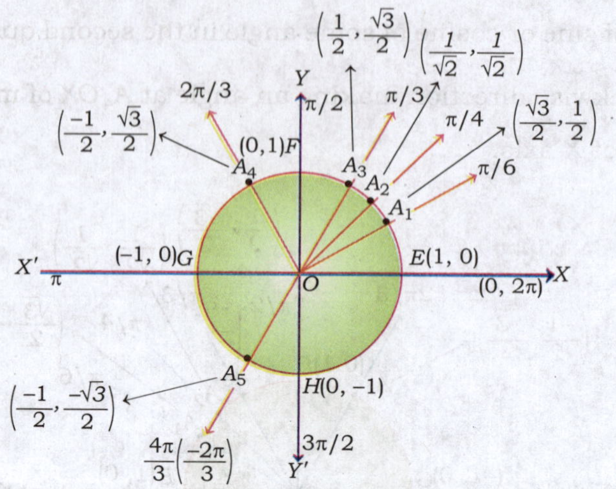

Fig. 7.3

6. To find the value of sine or cosine of some angle in the fourth quadrant, (say) $\frac{7\pi}{4}$, rotate the needle in anti-clockwise direction making an angle of $\frac{7\pi}{4}$ with the positive direction of X-axis represented by OA_6, as shown in Fig. (7.4). Angle $\frac{7\pi}{4}$ in anti-clockwise direction = Angle $-\frac{\pi}{4}$ in the clockwise direction.

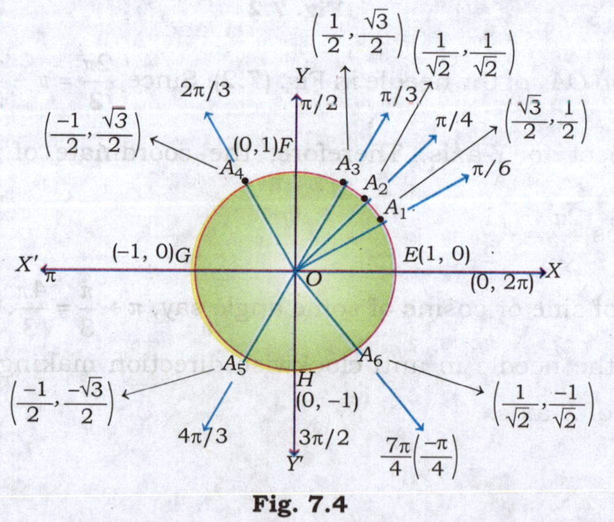

Fig. 7.4

7. From Fig. (7.4), A_6 is the mirror image of A_2 with respect to X-axis. Therefore, coordinates of A_6 are $\left(\frac{1}{\sqrt{2}}, -\frac{1}{\sqrt{2}}\right)$.

Thus, $\sin\left(\frac{7\pi}{4}\right) = \sin\left(-\frac{\pi}{4}\right) = -\frac{1}{\sqrt{2}}$ and $\cos\left(\frac{7\pi}{4}\right) = \cos\left(-\frac{\pi}{4}\right) = \frac{1}{\sqrt{2}}$

8. To find the value of sine or cosine of some angle, which is greater than one revolution, (say) $\frac{13\pi}{6}$, rotate the needle in anti-clockwise direction since $\frac{13\pi}{6} = 2\pi + \frac{\pi}{6}$, the needle will reach at the position OA_1. Therefore, $\sin\left(\frac{13\pi}{6}\right) = \sin\left(\frac{\pi}{6}\right) = \frac{1}{2}$ and $\cos\left(\frac{13\pi}{6}\right) = \cos\left(\frac{\pi}{6}\right) = \frac{\sqrt{3}}{2}$.

Observation

1. Angle made by the needle in one complete revolution is ....
2. $\cos\frac{\pi}{6} = \ldots\ldots\ldots = \cos\left(-\frac{\pi}{6}\right)$, $\sin\frac{\pi}{6} = \ldots\ldots\ldots = \sin(2\pi + \ldots)$.
3. Sine function is non-negative in ...... and ...... quadrants.
4. Cosine function is non-negative in ...... and .... quadrants.

Result

We have learnt how to find the values of sine and cosine functions in second, third and fourth quadrants using their given values in first quadrant.

Application

1. This activity can be used to get the values for tan, cot, sec, and cosec functions also.
2. From this activity students may learn that $\sin(-\theta) = -\sin\theta$ and $\cos(-\theta) = \cos\theta$.

   This activity can be applied to other trigonometric functions also.

Necessary Concepts Related to Activity

Sign of Trigonometric Functions in Different Quadrants

Let $X'OX$ and YOY' be the coordinate axes. Draw a circle with centre at origin O and radius unity. Suppose the circle cuts the coordinate axes at A, B, A' and B' as shown in Fig. (7.5).

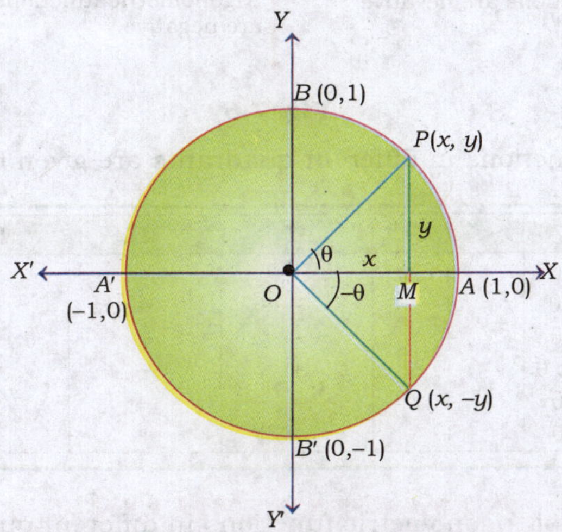

Fig. 7.5

Let $P(x, y)$ be a point on the circle such that $\angle AOP = \theta$. Then, $x = \cos\theta$ and $y = \sin\theta$.

If $\angle AOQ = -\theta$, then the coordinates of the point Q will be $(x, -y)$.

Therefore, $\cos(-\theta) = \cos\theta$ and $\sin(-\theta) = -\sin\theta$

Since, for every point $P(x, y)$ on the unit circle,

$-1 \le x \le 1$ and $-1 \le y \le 1 \Rightarrow -1 \le \cos\theta \le 1$ and $-1 \le \sin\theta \le 1$ for all values of θ.

Now, we know that in first quadrant $\left(\text{i.e. } 0 < \theta < \frac{\pi}{2}\right)$, x and y are both positive.

In the second quadrant (i.e. $\frac{\pi}{2} < \theta < \pi$), x is negative and y is positive.

In the third quadrant $\left(\text{i.e. } \pi < \theta < \frac{3\pi}{2}\right)$, x and y are both negative.

In the fourth quadrant $\left(\text{i.e. } \frac{3\pi}{2} < \theta < 2\pi\right)$, x is positive and y is negative.

According to this, we have $\sin\theta$ (i.e. y) is positive for $0 < \theta < \pi$ (i.e. in I and II quadrants) and negative for $\pi < \theta < 2\pi$ (i.e. in III and IV quadrants).

Similarly, $\cos\theta$ (i.e. x) is positive for $0 < x < \frac{\pi}{2}$ and $\frac{3\pi}{2} < x < 2\pi$ (i.e. in I and IV quadrants) and negative for $\frac{\pi}{2} < x < \frac{3\pi}{2}$ (i.e. in II and III quadrants).

Thus, we can find the signs of other trigonometric functions in different quadrants, which are given below in quadrant form and in table form.

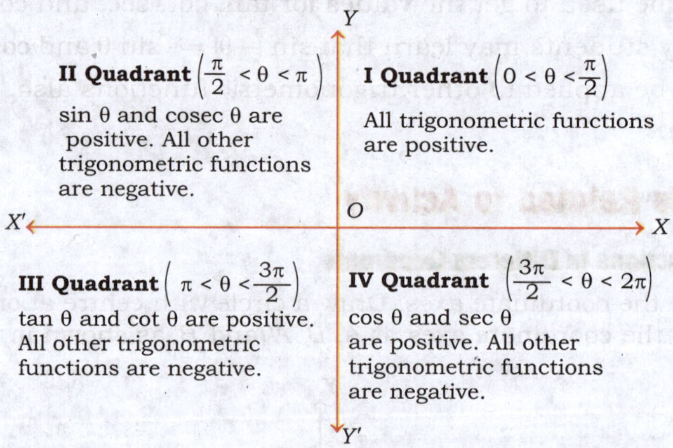

Fig. 7.6

The signs of trigonometric functions in different quadrants are given below

	I	II	III	IV
$\sin\theta$	+	+	−	−
$\cos\theta$	+	−	−	+
$\tan\theta$	+	−	+	−
$\text{cosec}\,\theta$	+	+	−	−
$\sec\theta$	+	−	−	+
$\cot\theta$	+	−	+	−

Note To remember the signs of trigonometric functions in different quadrants, we use the following four word phrase ' All School to College'. Here,

All → Indicate that all trigonometric functions are positive in I quadrant.

School → Indicate that sine and its reciprocal are positive in II quadrant.

To → Indicate that tan and its reciprocal are positive in III quadrant.

College → Indicate that cosine and its reciprocal are positive in IV quadrant.

Viva-Voce

Q.1 **In IV quadrant, sin x increases from -1 to 0 as x increases from $\frac{3\pi}{2}$ to 2π. Is it true or false?**

Ans True

Q.2 **$\cos(-x) =$ ....**

Ans $\cos x$

Q.3 **$\tan(\pi + x) = -\tan x$. Is it true or false?**

Ans False

Q.4 **If $\sin\theta = \frac{-5}{7}$ and θ lies in second quadrant, then find the value of $\cos\theta$.**

Ans $\cos\theta = \pm\sqrt{1-\sin^2\theta}$

$$= \pm\sqrt{1-\left(\frac{-5}{7}\right)^2} = \pm\sqrt{\frac{24}{49}} = \pm\frac{2\sqrt{6}}{7}$$

$\because$ $\cos\theta$ is negative in second quadrant.

$\therefore \cos\theta = -\frac{2\sqrt{6}}{7}$

Q.5 **If $\cos\theta = \frac{4}{5}$ and θ lies in the first quadrant. Then, find the value of $\sin\theta$.**

Ans $\sin\theta = \pm\sqrt{1-\cos^2\theta} = \pm\sqrt{1-\left(\frac{4}{5}\right)^2}$

$$= \pm\sqrt{1-\frac{16}{25}} = \pm\sqrt{\frac{9}{25}} = \pm\sqrt{\frac{9}{25}} = \pm\frac{3}{5}$$

$\because$ $\sin\theta$ is positive in first quadrant.

$\therefore \sin\theta = \frac{3}{5}$

Q.6 **Find the value of $\sin\theta$, if $\cos\theta = -\frac{\sqrt{3}}{2}$ and θ lies in third quadrant.**

Ans $\sin\theta = \pm\sqrt{1-\cos^2\theta} = \pm\sqrt{1-\left(-\frac{\sqrt{3}}{2}\right)^2}$

$$= \pm\sqrt{1-\frac{3}{4}} = \pm\sqrt{\frac{1}{4}} = \pm\frac{1}{2}$$

$\because$ $\sin\theta$ is negative in third quadrant.

$\therefore \sin\theta = -\frac{1}{2}$

Q.7 **Find the value of $\cos\theta$, if $\sin\theta = \frac{12}{13}$ and θ lies in the fourth quadrant**

Ans $\cos\theta = \pm\sqrt{1-\sin^2\theta}$

$$= \pm\sqrt{1-\left(\frac{12}{13}\right)^2} = \pm\sqrt{1-\frac{144}{169}}$$

$$= \pm\sqrt{\frac{25}{169}} = \pm\frac{5}{13}$$

$\because$ $\cos\theta$ is positive in fourth quadrant.

$\therefore \cos\theta = \frac{5}{13}$

Q.8 **Find the value of $\cot\theta$, if $\sin\theta = \frac{3}{5}$ and $\pi < \theta < \frac{3\pi}{2}$.**

Ans $\because \cot\theta = \frac{\cos\theta}{\sin\theta}$

$$\cos\theta = \pm\sqrt{1-\sin^2\theta} = \pm\sqrt{1-\left(\frac{3}{5}\right)^2} = \pm\sqrt{1-\frac{9}{25}}$$

$$= \pm\frac{4}{5}$$

$\because$ In third quadrant, $\cos\theta$ and $\cot\theta$ are negative and positive, respectively.

$\therefore \cos\theta = -\frac{4}{5}$ and $\cot\theta = -\frac{4/5}{3/5} = \frac{-4}{3}$

Q.9 **Find the value of $\sec\theta$, if $\sin\theta = \frac{1}{2}$ and $\frac{3\pi}{2} < \theta < 2\pi$.**

Ans $\because \sec\theta = \frac{1}{\cos\theta}$

$\therefore \cos\theta = \pm\sqrt{1-\sin^2\theta}$

$$= \pm\sqrt{1-\left(\frac{1}{2}\right)^2} = \pm\sqrt{1-\frac{1}{4}}$$

$$= \pm\frac{\sqrt{3}}{2}$$

$\because$ In fourth quadrant, $\cos\theta$ and $\sec\theta$ are positive.

$\therefore \cos = \frac{\sqrt{3}}{2}$ and $\sec\theta = \frac{1}{\frac{\sqrt{3}}{2}} = \frac{2}{\sqrt{3}}$

Activity 8

OBJECTIVE

To prepare a model to illustrate the values of sine function and cosine function for different angles which are multiples of $\pi/2$ and π.

Material Required

A stand fitted with 0° to 360° protractor and a circular plastic sheet fixed with handle which can be rotated at the centre of the protractor.

Prerequisite Knowledge

Concept of allied angles.

Method of Construction

1. First, take a stand fitted with 0° to 360° protractor.
2. Take the radius of protractor = 1 unit.

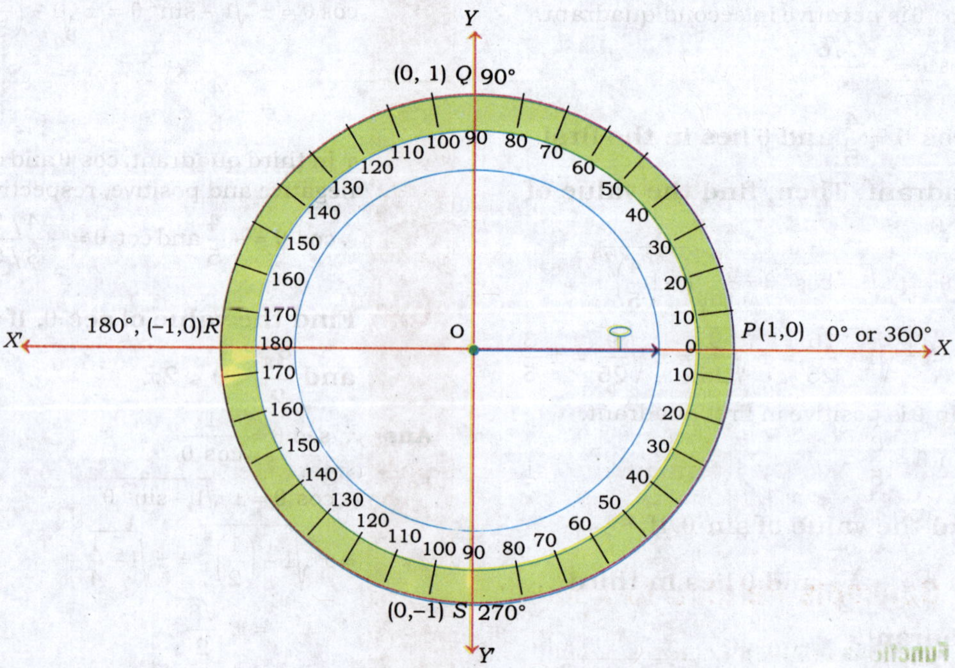

Fig. 8.1

3. Draw two perpendicular lines, one joining 0° to 180° line and another 90° to 270° line.
4. Mark the ends of 0° to 180° line as (1, 0) at 0°, (–1, 0) at 180° and that of 90° to 270° line as (0, 1) at 90° (0, –1) at 270°.
5. Take a plastic circular plate and mark a line to indicate its radius and fix a handle at the outer end of the radius.
6. Fix the plastic circular plate at the centre of the protractor.

Demonstration

1. Move the circular plate in anti-clockwise direction to make different angles like 0, $\frac{\pi}{2}$, π, $\frac{3\pi}{2}$, 2π, etc.
2. Read the values of sine and cosine function for these angles and their multiples from the perpendicular lines.

Observation

1. When radius line of circular plate is at 0° indicating the point P (1, 0), $\cos 0° =$ .... and $\sin 0° =$ ....
2. When radius line of circular plate is at 90° indicating the point Q (0, 1), $\cos\frac{\pi}{2} =$ .... and $\sin\frac{\pi}{2} =$ ....
3. When radius line of circular plate is at 180° indicating the point R (–1, 0), $\cos\pi =$ .... and $\sin\pi =$ ....
4. When radius line of circular plate is at 270° indicating the point S (0, –1), which means $\cos\frac{3\pi}{2} =$ .... and $\sin\frac{3\pi}{2} =$ ....
5. When radius line of circular plate is at 360° indicating the point again at P (1, 0), $\cos 2\pi =$ .... and $\sin 2\pi =$ ....

Now, fill in the table

Trigonometric function	0	$\frac{\pi}{2}$	π	$\frac{3\pi}{2}$	2π	$\frac{5\pi}{2}$	3π	$\frac{7\pi}{2}$	4π
$\sin\theta$									
$\cos\theta$									

Result We have learnt how to find the values of sine and cosine function for different angles which are multiples of $\frac{\pi}{2}$ and π.

Application

This activity can be used to determine the values of other trigonometric functions for angles being multiple of $\frac{\pi}{2}$ and π.

Necessary Concepts Related to Activity

Trigonometric Functions of Allied Angles

Two angles are said to be allied when their sum or difference is either zero or a multiple of $\pi/2$. The angles $-\theta$, $\frac{\pi}{2}\pm\theta$, $\pi\pm\theta$, $\frac{3\pi}{2}\pm\theta$, $2\pi\pm\theta$, etc. are angles allied to the angle θ, if θ is measured in radians.

The trigonometric functions changes at allied angles which are given in the following table

Allied angle/ Trigonometric function	sin θ	cosec θ	cos θ	sec θ	tan θ	cot θ
$-\theta$	$-\sin\theta$	$-\text{cosec}\,\theta$	$\cos\theta$	$\sec\theta$	$-\tan\theta$	$-\cot\theta$
$\pi/2-\theta$	$\cos\theta$	$\sec\theta$	$\sin\theta$	$\text{cosec}\,\theta$	$\cot\theta$	$\tan\theta$
$\pi/2+\theta$	$\cos\theta$	$\sec\theta$	$-\sin\theta$	$-\text{cosec}\,\theta$	$-\cot\theta$	$-\tan\theta$
$\pi-\theta$	$\sin\theta$	$\text{cosec}\,\theta$	$-\cos\theta$	$-\sec\theta$	$-\tan\theta$	$-\cot\theta$
$\pi+\theta$	$-\sin\theta$	$-\text{cosec}\,\theta$	$-\cos\theta$	$-\sec\theta$	$\tan\theta$	$\cot\theta$
$3\pi/2-\theta$	$-\cos\theta$	$-\sec\theta$	$-\sin\theta$	$-\text{cosec}\,\theta$	$\cot\theta$	$\tan\theta$
$3\pi/2+\theta$	$-\cos\theta$	$-\sec\theta$	$\sin\theta$	$\text{cosec}\,\theta$	$-\cot\theta$	$-\tan\theta$
$2\pi-\theta$	$-\sin\theta$	$-\text{cosec}\,\theta$	$\cos\theta$	$\sec\theta$	$-\tan\theta$	$-\cot\theta$
$2\pi+\theta$	$\sin\theta$	$\text{cosec}\,\theta$	$\cos\theta$	$\sec\theta$	$\tan\theta$	$\cot\theta$

Method to Find the Values of Trigonometric Function having Allied Angles

We know the values of trigonometric functions for acute angles and values for allied angles are not easy to remember, so we find the value of trigonometric functions having allied angles by using the following steps

***Step* I** Firstly check the given angle say α is positive or negative. If it is negative, then make it positive by using the following suitable formula.

$$\sin(-\alpha) = -\sin\alpha,\ \cos(-\alpha) = \cos\alpha,\ \tan(-\alpha) = -\tan\alpha$$

***Step* II** Write the positive angle α obtained from Step I as a multiple of $\frac{\pi}{2}$, i.e. in the form $\alpha = \frac{\pi}{2} \times n \pm \theta$, where θ is an acute angle.

***Step* III** If n in Step II is an odd integer, then convert the trigonometric function by using $\sin\alpha = \pm\cos\theta$, $\cos\alpha = \pm\sin\theta$, $\tan\alpha = \pm\cot\theta$, $\sec\alpha = \pm\text{cosec}\,\theta$ and $\text{cosec}\,\alpha = \pm\sec\theta$

If n in Step II is an even integer, then convert the trigonometric function by using $\sin\alpha = \pm\sin\theta$, $\cos\alpha = \pm\cos\theta$, $\tan\alpha = \pm\tan\theta$, $\sec\alpha = \pm\sec\theta$ and $\text{cosec}\,\alpha = \pm\text{cosec}\,\theta$

***Step* IV** Determine the quadrant in which α lies and take the sign of trigonometrical function obtained in Step III in that quadrant and write the value of trigonometric function for acute angle θ.

Viva-Voce

Q.1 If θ is measured in radian, then the angles allied to θ are θ, $\frac{\pi}{2} \pm \theta$, $\pi \pm \theta$, $2\pi \pm \theta$, etc. Is it true or false?

Ans True

Q.2 Explain about the 'allied angles'.

Ans Two angles are said to be allied when their sum or difference is either zero or a multiple of 90°.

Q.3 Write the trigonometric functions having positive signs in second quadrant.

Ans sin θ and cosec θ

Q.4 Trigonometric functions for (2π + θ) and (2nπ + θ) are not same as those for θ, where $n \in Z$. Is it true or false?

Ans False

Q.5 The value of $\cos\left(\frac{41\pi}{4}\right)$ is $\frac{1}{\sqrt{2}}$. Is it true or false?

Ans True

Q.6 Write the least value of $\cos^2\theta + \sec^2\theta$.

Ans 2

Q.7 If $\tan\theta = -\frac{1}{\sqrt{5}}$ and θ lies in the fourth quadrant, then the value of cos θ is ……… .

Ans $\frac{\sqrt{5}}{\sqrt{6}}$

Activity 9

OBJECTIVE

To plot the graphs of sin x, sin$2x$, 2sin$x$ and sin$\frac{x}{2}$, using same coordinate axes.

Material Required

Plyboard, squared paper, gum, ruler, different coloured pens, eraser.

Prerequisite Knowledge

Concept of values of trigonometric functions of some standard angles.

Method of Construction

1. First, take a plyboard of size 40 cm × 40 cm.
2. On the plyboard, paste a thick graph paper of size 30 cm × 30 cm.
3. Draw two mutually perpendicular lines on the squared paper, and take them as coordinate axes.
4. Graduate the two axes as shown in the Fig. (9.1).
5. Prepare the table of ordered pairs for sin x, sin $2x$, 2 sin x and sin $\frac{x}{2}$ for different value of x as shown in the table below:

Trigonometric ratios	0°	$\frac{\pi}{12}$	$\frac{\pi}{6}$	$\frac{\pi}{4}$	$\frac{\pi}{3}$	$\frac{5\pi}{12}$	$\frac{\pi}{2}$	$\frac{7\pi}{12}$	$\frac{2\pi}{3}$	$\frac{9\pi}{12}$	$\frac{5\pi}{6}$	$\frac{11\pi}{12}$	π
sin x	0	0.26	0.50	0.71	0.86	0.97	1.00	0.97	0.86	0.71	0.50	0.26	0
sin $2x$	0	0.50	0.86	1.00	0.86	0.50	0	– 0.5	– 0.86	– 1.0	– 0.86	– 0.50	0
2 sin x	0	0.52	1.00	1.42	1.72	1.94	2.00	1.94	1.72	1.42	1.00	0.52	0
sin $\frac{x}{2}$	0	0.13	0.26	0.38	0.50	0.61	0.71	0.79	0.86	0.92	0.97	0.99	1.00

Demonstration

Plot the ordered pair (x, sin x), (x, sin$2x$), $\left(x, \sin\frac{x}{2}\right)$ and (x, 2sin x) on the same coordinate axes and join the plotted ordered pairs by free hand curves in different colours as shown in the Fig. (9.1).

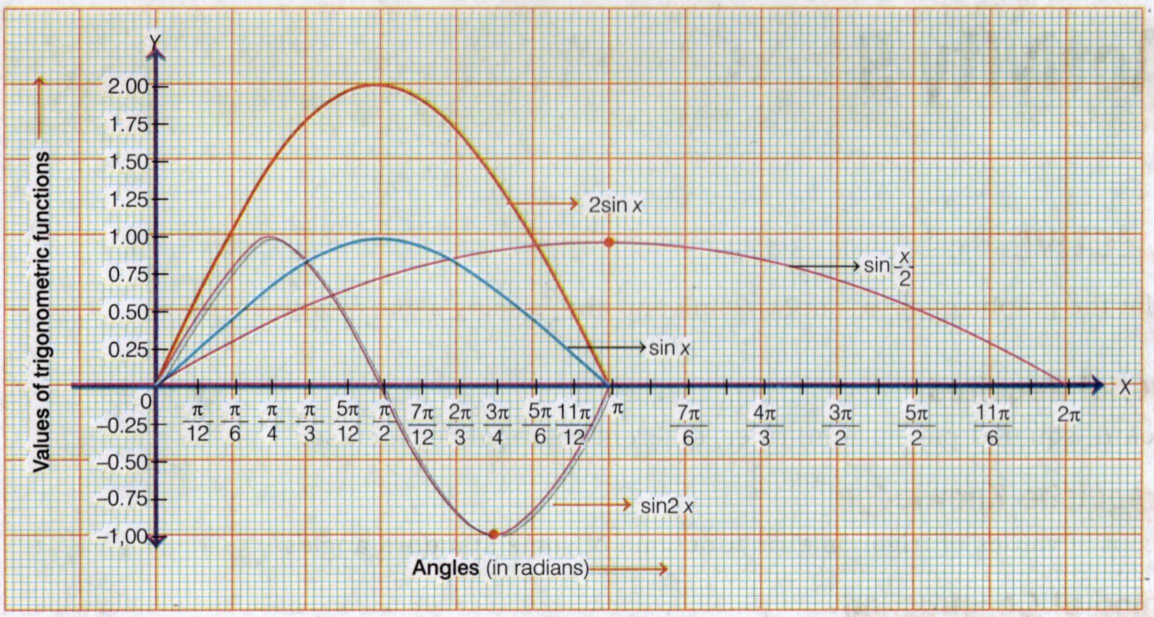

Fig. 9.1

Observation

1. Graphs of $\sin x$ and $2\sin x$ are of same shape but the maximum height of the graph of $\sin x$ is .... the maximum height of the graph of ....
2. The maximum height of the graph of $\sin 2x$ is .... It is at $x =$ ....
3. The maximum height of the graph of $2\sin x$ is .... It is at $x =$ ....
4. The maximum height of the graph of $\sin\frac{x}{2}$ is .... It is at $\frac{x}{2} =$ ....
5. At $x =$ .... , $\sin x = 0$, at $x =$ .... , $\sin 2x = 0$ and $x =$ ...., $\sin\frac{x}{2} = 0$.
6. In the interval $[0, \pi]$, graphs of $\sin x$, $2\sin x$ and $\sin\frac{x}{2}$ are .... X-axis and some portion of the graph of $\sin 2x$ lies .... X-axis.
7. Graphs of $\sin x$ and $\sin 2x$ intersect at $x =$ .... in the interval $(0, \pi)$.
8. Graphs of $\sin x$ and $\sin\frac{x}{2}$ intersect at $x =$ ...... in the interval $(0, \pi)$.

Result

We have learnt how to plot the graph of $\sin x$, $\sin 2x$, $2\sin x$ and $\sin\frac{x}{2}$, using same coordinate axes.

Application

This activity may be used in comparing graphs of a trigonometric function of multiples and sub-multiples of angles.

Necessary Concepts Related to Activity

To draw the graph of any function, we should know the values of function at different points.

Trigonometric Functions of Some Standard Angles

Values of trigonometric functions at some angles are given below. With the help of these values, we can draw their graphs

Angle \ θ	sin θ	cos θ	tan θ	cot θ	sec θ	cosec θ
0°	0	1	0	∞	1	∞
$30°\left(\frac{\pi}{6}\right)$	$\frac{1}{2}$	$\frac{\sqrt{3}}{2}$	$\frac{1}{\sqrt{3}}$	$\sqrt{3}$	$\frac{2}{\sqrt{3}}$	2
$45°\left(\frac{\pi}{4}\right)$	$\frac{1}{\sqrt{2}}$	$\frac{1}{\sqrt{2}}$	1	1	$\sqrt{2}$	$\sqrt{2}$
$60°\left(\frac{\pi}{3}\right)$	$\frac{\sqrt{3}}{2}$	$\frac{1}{2}$	$\sqrt{3}$	$\frac{1}{\sqrt{3}}$	2	$\frac{2}{\sqrt{3}}$
$90°\left(\frac{\pi}{2}\right)$	1	0	∞	0	∞	1
$120°\left(\frac{2\pi}{3}\right)$	$\frac{\sqrt{3}}{2}$	$-\frac{1}{2}$	$-\sqrt{3}$	$-\frac{1}{\sqrt{3}}$	−2	$\frac{2}{\sqrt{3}}$
$135°\left(\frac{3\pi}{4}\right)$	$\frac{1}{\sqrt{2}}$	$-\frac{1}{\sqrt{2}}$	−1	−1	$-\sqrt{2}$	$\sqrt{2}$
$150°\left(\frac{5\pi}{6}\right)$	$\frac{1}{2}$	$-\frac{\sqrt{3}}{2}$	$-\frac{1}{\sqrt{3}}$	$-\sqrt{3}$	$-\frac{2}{\sqrt{3}}$	2
180° (π)	0	−1	0	−∞	−1	∞
$270°\left(\frac{3\pi}{2}\right)$	−1	0	∞	0	∞	−1
360° (2π)	0	1	0	∞	1	∞

Note Here, the symbol '∞' is used for not defined.

Viva-Voce

Q.1 Write the period of sin x.

Ans 2π

Q.2 'Trigonometric ratios are same for the same angle', is it true?

Ans No, trigonometric ratios are not same for the same angle.

Q.3 The period of $\sin(ax + b)$ is $\frac{2\pi}{a}$. Is it true or false?

Ans True

Q.4 On the graph of $y = 3\sin x$. The minimum value of y is ....

Ans −3

Q.5 On the graph of $y = c\sin ax$. The maximum value of y is ....

Ans c

Q.6 $\sin 1° > \sin 1$, is it true?

Ans No, it is false. Since, $\sin 1° < \sin 1$.

Q.7 Write the period of $\sin\left(\frac{x}{2}\right)$.

Ans 4π

Q.8 In order to draw the graph of $y = 4\sin 2x$, we draw the graph of $y = \sin x$ and on X-axis change k to $\frac{k}{2}$. Is it true or false?

Ans True

Q.9 Write the value of $\tan\left(\frac{19\pi}{3}\right)$.

Ans We have, $\frac{19\pi}{3} = \left(\frac{19}{3} \times 180\right)^\circ$

$= 1140° = 90° \times 12 + 60°$

Clearly, the angle lies in first quadrant.

$\therefore \tan\left(\frac{19\pi}{3}\right) = \tan(90° \times 12 + 60°)$

$= \tan 60° = \sqrt{3}$

Activity 10

OBJECTIVE

To interpret geometrically, the meaning of $i = \sqrt{-1}$ and its integral powers.

Material Required

Drawing board, white sheet, different coloured pens, ruler, compasses, glue, pins, thread etc.

Prerequisite knowledge

1. Concept of iota.
2. Concept of properties of iota.

Method of Construction

1. Take a drawing board of suitable size and fix a white sheet on it.
2. Draw two mutually perpendicular lines $X'X$ and YY' intersecting at the point O (shown given below Fig. (10.1)).

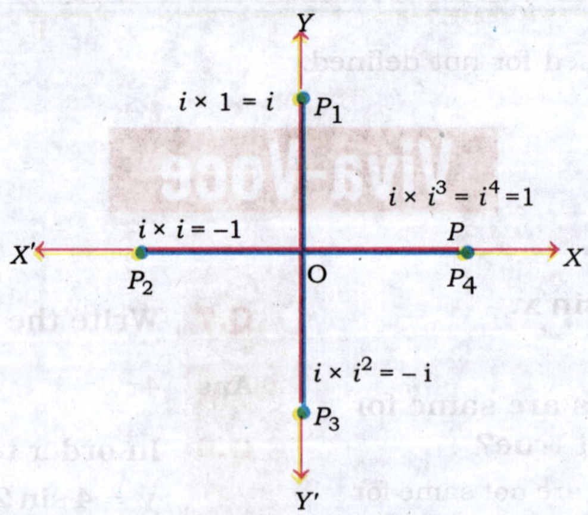

Fig. 10.1

3. Take a thread of a unit length representing the number 1 along OX. Fix one end of the thread to the pin at O and the other end at P as shown in the Fig. (10.1).
4. Set free the other end of the thread at P and rotate the thread through angles of 90°, 180°, 270° and 360° and mark the free end of the thread in different cases as P_1, P_2, P_3 and P_4, respectively, as shown in the Fig. (10.1).

Demonstration

1. In the argand plane, OP, OP_1, OP_2, OP_3, OP_4 represent, respectively, 1, i, – 1, – i, 1.
2. $OP_1 = i = 1 \times i$, $OP_2 = -1 = i \times i = i^2$, $OP_3 = -i = i \times i \times i = i^3$ and so on.

   Each time, rotation of OP by 90° is equivalent to multiplication by i. Thus, i is referred to as the multiplying factor for a rotation of 90°.

Observation

1. On rotating OP through 90°, $OP_1 = 1 \times i = \ldots\ldots$.
2. On rotating OP through an angle of 180°, $OP_2 = 1 \times \ldots \times \ldots = \ldots\ldots$.
3. On rotating of OP through 270° (3 right angles), $OP_3 = 1 \times \ldots \times \ldots \times \ldots = \ldots\ldots$.
4. On rotating OP through 360° (4 right angles), $OP_4 = 1 \times \ldots \times \ldots \times \ldots \times \ldots = \ldots\ldots$.
5. On rotating OP through n-right angles, $OP_n = 1 \times \ldots \times \ldots \times \ldots \times \ldots \times \ldots$ n-times $= \ldots\ldots$.

Result

We have learnt geometrical meaning of i (iota) and its integral powers.

Application

This activity may be used to evaluate any integral power of i.

Necessary Concepts Related to Activity

1. Iota (i)

Euler (1707-1743) was the first mathematician, who introduced the symbol i (read as iota) for $\sqrt{-1}$ with property $i^2 + 1 = 0$, i.e. $i^2 = -1$. He also called this symbol as the imaginary unit.

2. Positive Integral Powers of i

We know that, $i = \sqrt{-1}$.

We can write higher powers of i as follows

(i) $i^0 = 1$

(ii) $(i)^1 = i$

(iii) $i^2 = -1$

(iv) $i^3 = i^2 \cdot i = -1 \times i = -i$

(v) $i^4 = (i^2)^2 = (-1)^2 = 1$

(vi) $i^{4q} = (i^4)^q = (1)^q = 1, q \in N$

(vii) $i^{4q+1} = (i^{4q})\, i^1 = 1 \times i = i, q \in N$

(viii) $i^{4q+2} = (i^{4q}) i^2 = 1 \times (-1) = -1, q \in N$

(ix) $i^{4q+3} = (i^{4q})\, i^3 = 1 \times i^3 = -i, q \in N$

3. Negative Integral Powers of i

The negative integral power of i, i.e. i^{-p} is rewritten as $\frac{1}{i^p}$ and then i^p is expressed as $i^p = i^{4q+r} = i^r$, where $q, r \in N$.

e.g. To compute i^{-15}, we write it as $\frac{1}{i^{15}}$.

$$\text{Then, } i^{-15} = \frac{1}{i^{15}} = \frac{1}{(i)^{4\times3+3}} = \frac{1}{(i^4)^3 \cdot i^3} = \frac{1}{(1)^3 \cdot i^3} = \frac{1}{-i} \times \frac{i}{i} \qquad [\because i^4 = 1]$$

$$= \frac{i}{(-i)\, i} = \frac{i}{-i^2} = \frac{i}{-(-1)} = \frac{i}{1} = i$$

Viva-Voce

Q.1 Name the mathematician, who introduced iota (i).

Ans Euler was the first mathematician, who introduced iota (i) for $\sqrt{-1}$ with the property $i^2 + 1 = 0$.

Q.2 $\sqrt{a} \times \sqrt{b} \neq \sqrt{ab}$, if both a and b are negative real numbers. Is it true or false?

Ans True

Q.3 $i^n + i^{n+1} + i^{n+2} + i^{n+3} = 0,\ \forall\ n \in N$. Is it true or false?

Ans True

Q.4 If n is an odd integer, $i = \sqrt{-1}$, then find the value of $(1+i)^{6n} + (1-i)^{6n}$.

Ans We have, $(1+i)^{6n} + (1-i)^{6n} = [(1+i)^2]^{3n} + [(1-i)^2]^{3n} = [1 + i^2 + 2i]^{3n} + [1 + i^2 - 2i]^{3n}$

$= (2i)^{3n} + (-2i)^{3n}$, as n is odd.

$\Rightarrow\ (2i)^{3n} - (2i)^{3n} = 0$

Q.5 Evaluate, $(-\sqrt{-1})^{4n+5}$, $n \in N$.

Ans We have, $(-\sqrt{-1})^{4n+5} = (-i)^{4n+5}$

$= (-i)^{4n} \cdot (-i)^5$

$= 1 \times (-i) = -i$

Q.6 Evaluate i^{13}.

Ans We have, $i^{13} = i^9 \cdot i^4$

$= (i^3)^3 \cdot (i^2)^2$

$= (-i)^3 \cdot (-1)^2 = i \times 1 = i$

Q.7 Find the value of the sum $\sum_{n=1}^{13} (i^n + i^{n+1})$.

Ans $\because$ The sum of any four consecutive powers of i is zero.

$\therefore \sum_{n=1}^{13} (i^n + i^{n+1}) = \sum_{n=1}^{13} i^n + \sum_{i=1}^{13} (i^{n+1})$

$= (i + i^2 + i^3 + \ldots + i^{13}) + (i^2 + i^3 + i^4 + \ldots + i^{14})$

$= (i + 0) + (i^2 + 0)$

$= i - 1$

Q.8 Evaluate $\left\{ i^{10} + \left(\frac{1}{i}\right)^{20} \right\}^5$.

Ans We have, $\left\{ i^{10} + \left(\frac{1}{i}\right)^{20} \right\}^5 = \left\{ i^8 . i^2 + \left(\frac{1}{i^{20}}\right) \right\}^5$

$= \{i^2 + 1\}^5$

$= \{-1 + 1\}^5$

$= 0$

Activity 11

OBJECTIVE

To find the number of ways in which three cards can be selected from given five cards.

Material Required

Drawing board, drawing sheet, coloured pens, cutter, etc.

Prerequisite Knowledge

1. Concept of factorial notation.
2. Concept of permutation.
3. Concept of combination.

Method of Construction

1. Take a drawing board and fix a drawing sheet on it.
2. Cut out five identical cards of suitable size from the drawing board.
3. Mark these cards as *P, Q, R, S* and *T*.

Demonstration

1. Select any three card from the given five cards.
2. Let the first selected card be *P*. Then other two cards from the remaining four cards can be : *QR, QS, QT, RS, RT* and *ST*. Thus, the possible selections are : *PQR, PQS, PQT, PRS, PRT* and *PST*. Record these on a drawing sheet.
3. Let the first selected card be *Q*. Then the other two cards from the remaining four cards can be : *PR, PS, PT, RS, RT* and *ST*. Thus, the possible selections are : *QPR, QPS, QPT, QRS, QRT* and *QST*. Record these on the same drawing sheet.
4. Let the first selected card be *R*. Then the other two cards can be : *PQ, PS, PT, QS, QT* and *ST*. Thus, the possible selections are : *RPQ, RPS, RPT, RQS, RQT* and *RST*. Record these on the same drawing sheet.
5. Let the first selected card be *S*. Then the other two cards can be : *PQ, PR, PT, QR, QT* and *RT*. Thus, the possible selections are : *SPQ, SPR, SPT, SQR, SQT* and *SRT*. Record these on the same drawing sheet.
6. Let the first selected card be *T*. Then the other two cards can be : *PQ, PR, PS, QR, QS* and *RS*. Thus, the possible selections are : *TPQ, TPR, TPS, TQR, TQS* and *TRS*. Record these on the same drawing sheet.
7. Now, look at the drawing sheet on which the possible selections are listed. Here, there are in all 30 possible selections and each of the selection is repeated thrice. Therefore, the number of distinct selection = $30 \div 3 = 10$ which is same as ${}^5C_3$.

Observation

1. *PQR, QPR* and *RPQ*, represent the ...... selections.
2. *PQS*, ... , ... represent the same selections.
3. Among *QPT, PQT, PQR*, ... and .... represent the same selections.
4. *QPT, PQR*, represent .... selections.
5. Among *RPT, PSR, TRS, SQT, QSR, PRT, RPT*, ... represent the same selections. *RPT, PST*, ..., ..., represent different selections.

Result

We have learnt how to find number of ways in which three cards can be selected from the given five cards.

Application

Activities of this type can be used in understanding the general formula for finding the number of possible selections when r objects are selected from given n distinct objects, i.e. ${}^nC_r = \frac{n!}{r!\,(n-r)!}$.

Necessary Concepts Related to Activity

1. Factorial Notation

Many times, we come across the products of the form 1×2, $1 \times 2 \times 3$, $1 \times 2 \times 3 \times 4$, ... For our convenience, we use a special notation instead of writing all the factors of such a product. We write

$$1! = 1$$

$$2! = 2 \times 1$$

$$3! = 3 \times 2 \times 1$$

....

....

$$n! = n(n-1)\,(n-2)\ldots 3 \cdot 2 \cdot 1$$

Thus, the continued product of first n natural numbers is called the 'n factorial' and is denoted by $n!$ or $\lfloor n$.

Also,

$$n! = n\,(n-1)!$$

$$= n\,(n-1)\,(n-2)! \quad \text{[provided } n \geq 2]$$

$$= n\,(n-1)\,(n-2)\,(n-3)! \quad \text{[provided } n \geq 3]$$

2. Permutations

The word permutation means an arrangement.

A permutation is an arrangement in a definite order of a number of objects taken some or all at a time. i.e. each of the arrangements which can be made by taking some or all of a number of objects is called a permutation. Thus, in permutation the order of arrangement is important. When the order is changed, a different permutation is obtained.

e.g. If there are three objects say A, B and C, then the permutations of these three objects taking two at a time are AB, BC, AC, BA, CB, CA.

So, number of permutations is 6.

Number of Permutations

The number of permutation of n different objects taken r at a time, where $0 < r \le n$ and the objects do not repeat, is $n(n-1)(n-2)\ldots(n-r+1)$, which is denoted by ${}^nP_r$ or $P(n, r)$.

$$ {}^nP_r = \frac{n!}{(n-r)!}, \quad 0 < r \le n $$

e.g. ${}^7P_4$ denotes the number of permutations of 7 things taken 4 at a time.

3. Combinations

The word combination means selection.

Each of the different groups or selection which can be made by taking some or all of a number of things or object at a time irrespective of their arrangements is called a combination.

In combination, the order is not important. Suppose twelve persons meet in a room and each shakes hand with all the others. X shaking hands with Y and Y with X, will not be two different hand shakes. Thus, order is not important here and here number of hand shakes will be equal to the combinations of 12 things taken 2 at a time.

e.g. The different combinations formed of three letters A, B, C taking two at a time are AB, AC, BC.

4. Meaning of ${}^nC_r$

The number of combinations of n different things taken r at a time means that the number of groups of r things which can be formed from n things and generally it is denoted by symbol ${}^nC_r$ or $C(n, r)$.

Viva-Voce

Q.1 Explain combination.

Ans Each of the different groups or selection which can be made by taking some or all of a number of things or object at a time, irrespective of their arrangements is called a combination.

Q.2 Calculate the number of all selections of n distinct things, taken r at a time.

Ans Required number of selections

$$ = {}^nC_r = \frac{n!}{r!\,(n-r)!} $$

Q.3 List the different combinations formed of three letters P, Q, R taken two at a time.

Ans PQ, QR and RP.

Q.4 Write the relation between $P(n, r)$ and $C(n, r)$.

Ans $P(n, r) = C(n, r)r!$ or ${}^nP_r = {}^nC_r \times r!$

Q.5 If ${}^nC_r = k \cdot {}^nC_{n-r}$, then find k.

Ans We know that, ${}^nC_r = {}^nC_{n-r}$

$\therefore \quad k = 1$

Q.6 If a polygon has n sides, then write number of its diagonals.

Ans If a polygon has n sides.

$\therefore$ Number of diagonals $= {}^nC_2 - n = \dfrac{n(n-3)}{2}$

Q.7 The number of permutations of n different objects taken r at a time, where repetition is allowed, is ....

Ans n^r

Q.8 The number of permutations of n objects, where p objects are of the same kind and rest are all different, is $\dfrac{n!}{p!}$. Is it true or false?

Ans True

Q.9 Evaluate ${}^{10}C_8$.

Ans We have, ${}^{10}C_8 = {}^{10}C_{10-8} = {}^{10}C_2 = \dfrac{10 \times 9}{2 \times 1} = 45$

Q.10 Write the value of ${}^nC_0$.

Ans We have, ${}^nC_0 = \dfrac{n!}{(n-0)!\,0!} = \dfrac{n!}{n!\,0!} = 1$

$[\because 0! = 1]$

Activity 12

OBJECTIVE

To construct a Pascal's Triangle and to write binomial expansion for a given positive integral exponent.

Material Required

Drawing board, white paper, some matchsticks, gum or fevistick, cutter, coloured pens, etc.

Prerequisite Knowledge

1. Concept of binomial expression.
2. Concept of binomial expansion.
3. Concept of binomial theorem.

Method of Construction

1. Take a drawing board and fix a white paper on it.
2. Take some matchsticks and arrange them as shown in Fig. (12.1)

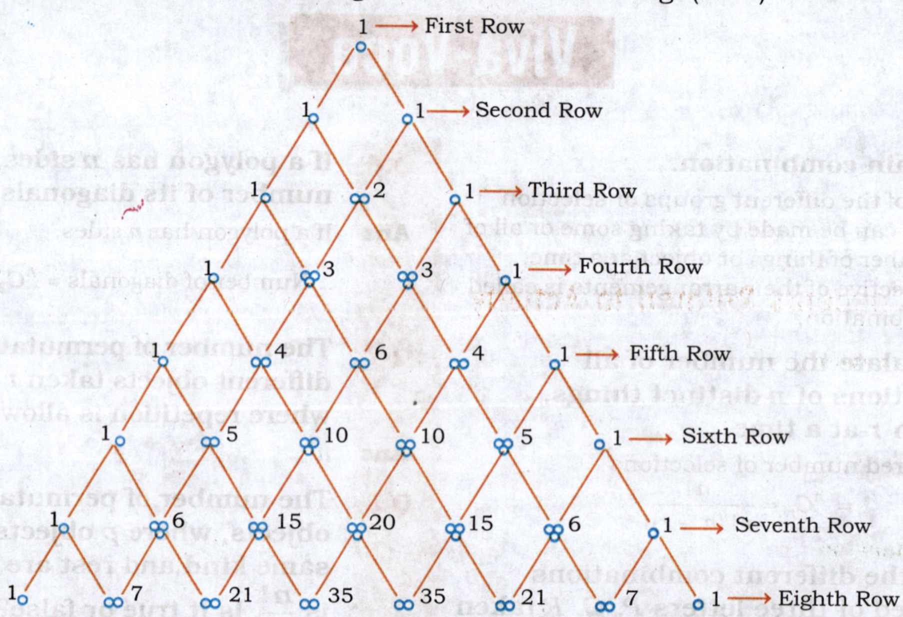

Fig. 12.1

3. Write the numbers as follows

1 (First Row)
1 1 (Second Row)
1 2 1 (Third Row)
1 3 3 1 (Fourth Row)
and so on (see Fig. 12.1)

Fig. 12.2

4. To write binomial expansion of $(a + b)^n$, use the numbers given in the $(n + 1)$th row.

Demonstration

1. The above figure looks like a triangle and is referred to as Pascal's triangle.
2. Numbers of the second row give the coefficients of the terms of the binomial expansion of $(a+b)^1$. Similarly, numbers in the third row give the coefficients of the terms of the binomial expansion of $(a+b)^2$, numbers in the fourth row give coefficients of the terms of binomial expansion of $(a+b)^3$. Again, numbers in the fifth row give the coefficients of the terms of binomial expansion of $(a+b)^4$ and so on.

Observation

1. Numbers in the fifth row are ......, which are coefficients of the binomial expansion of...... .
2. Numbers in the seventh row are ......, which are coefficients of the binomial expansion of ....
3. $(a+b)^3 = \ldots a^3 + \ldots a^2b + \ldots ab^2 + \ldots . b^3$
4. $(a+b)^5 = \ldots + \ldots + \ldots + \ldots + \ldots + \ldots .$
5. $(a+b)^6 = \ldots a^6 + \ldots a^5b + \ldots a^4b^2 + \ldots a^3b^3 + \ldots a^2b^4 + \ldots ab^5 + \ldots b^6.$
6. $(a+b)^8 = \ldots + \ldots + \ldots + \ldots + \ldots + \ldots + \ldots + \ldots + \ldots .$
7. $(a+b)^{10} = \ldots + \ldots + \ldots + \ldots + \ldots + \ldots + \ldots + \ldots + \ldots + \ldots + \ldots .$

Result

We have learnt how to construct a Pascal's triangle and to write binomial expansion for a given positive integral exponent.

Application

This activity can be used to find general term in a binomial expansion for $(a+b)^n$, where n is a positive integer.

Necessary Concepts Related to Activity

1. Binomial Expression

An algebraic expression consisting of two terms with +ve or –ve sign between them, is called binomial expression. e.g. $(a+2b)$, $\left(\frac{p}{x^2}-\frac{q}{x^4}\right)$, $\left(3x-\frac{2}{y}\right)$

2. Binomial Expansion

In earlier classes, we have already studied that

(i) $(a+b)^0 = 1$

(ii) $(a+b)^1 = a+b$

(iii) $(a+b)^2 = a^2+2ab+b^2$

(iv) $(a+b)^3 = a^3+3a^2b+3ab^2+b^3$

(v) $(a+b)^4 = a^4+4a^3b+6a^2b^2+4ab^3+b^4$

In these expansions, we observe that

(i) The total number of terms in the expansion is one more than the index.

(ii) Powers of the first quantity 'a' decreases by 1, whereas the powers of the second quantity 'b' increases by 1, in the successive terms.

(iii) In each term of the expansion, the sum of indices of a and b is the same and is equal to the index of $(a+b)$.

Thus, the coefficient of variables in the above expansions follow a particular pattern, which is given below

Index of the binomial	Coefficients of various terms	Expansion
0	1	$(a+b)^0 = 1$
1	1 ▽ 1	$(a+b)^1 = a + b$ i.e. 1 1
2	1 ▽ 2 ▽ 1	$(a+b)^2 = a^2 + 2ab + b^2$ i.e. 1 2 1
3	1 ▽ 3 ▽ 3 ▽ 1	$(a+b)^3 = a^3 + 3a^2b + 3ab^2 + b^3$ i.e. 1 3 3 1
4	1 ▽ 4 ▽ 6 ▽ 4 ▽ 1	$(a+b)^4 = a^4 + 4a^3b + 6a^2b^2 + 4ab^3 + b^4$ i.e. 1 4 6 4 1
5	1 ▽ 5 ▽ 10 ▽ 10 ▽ 5 ▽ 1	$(a+b)^5 = a^5 + 5a^4b + 10a^3b^2 + 10a^2b^3 + 5ab^4 + b^5$ i.e. 1 5 10 10 5 1

It can also be seen from the pattern that the addition of 1's in the row for index 1 gives rise to 2 in the row for index 2. The addition of 1, 2 and 2, 1 in the row for index 2 gives rise to 3 and 3 in the row for index 3 and so on. Also each row is bounded by 1 on both sides.

3. Binomial Theorem for any Positive Integer

If a and b are two real numbers, then for any positive integer n, we have

$$(a+b)^n = {}^nC_0a^nb^0 + {}^nC_1a^{n-1}b^1 + {}^nC_2a^{n-2}b^2 + \cdots + {}^nC_na^0b^n$$

$$= {}^nC_0a^n + {}^nC_1a^{n-1}b + {}^nC_2a^{n-2}b^2 + \cdots + {}^nC_nb^n$$

$$\Rightarrow \quad (a+b)^n = \sum_{r=0}^{n} {}^nC_ra^{n-r}b^r$$

where, ${}^nC_0, {}^nC_1, \ldots, {}^nC_n$ are called binomial coefficients. These binomial coefficients can be rewritten as $C_0, C_1, \ldots, C_n$.

Viva-Voce

Q.1 Explain binomial expression.

Ans An algebraic expression consisting of two terms with positive or negative sign between them, is called binomial expression.

Q.2 State binomial theorem.

Ans If a and b are two real numbers, then for any positive integer n, we have

$$(a+b)^n = {}^nC_0a^nb^0 + {}^nC_1a^{n-1}b^1 + {}^nC_2a^{n-2}b^2 + \ldots + {}^nC_na^0b^n$$

Q.3 Define Pascal's triangle.

Ans The structure which is used to understand and remember the coefficients of variables in any expansion, looks like a triangle with 1 at the top vertex and running down the two slanting sides. This structure or array of numbers, is known as Pascal's triangle.

Q.4 Write the number of terms in the expansion of $(a+b)^n$.

Ans Number of terms in the expansion of $(a+b)^n$ is $n+1$.

Q.5 Write the sum of the indices of a and b in the each term of the expansion of $(a+b)^n$.

Ans In each term of the expansion, the sum of the indices of a and b is always equal to n.

Q.6 Write the general term of the expansion $(a+b)^n$.

Ans General term, $T_{r+1} = {}^nC_r\, a^{n-r}b^r$

Q.8 Write the binomial coefficients of the expansion $(x+y)^5$.

Ans ${}^5C_0, {}^5C_1, {}^5C_2, {}^5C_3, {}^5C_4, {}^5C_5$

Activity 13

OBJECTIVE

To demonstrate that the Arithmetic mean of two different positive numbers is always greater than the Geometric mean.

Material Required

Coloured sheet, scale, coloured pens, cutter etc.

Prerequisite Knowledge

1. Concept of Arithmetic mean.
2. Concept of Geometric mean.
3. Concept of relation between AM and GM.

Method of Construction

1. From coloured sheet, cut off four rectangular pieces of dimension $a \times b$ $(a > b)$.
2. Arrange the four rectangular pieces as shown in Fig. (13.1).

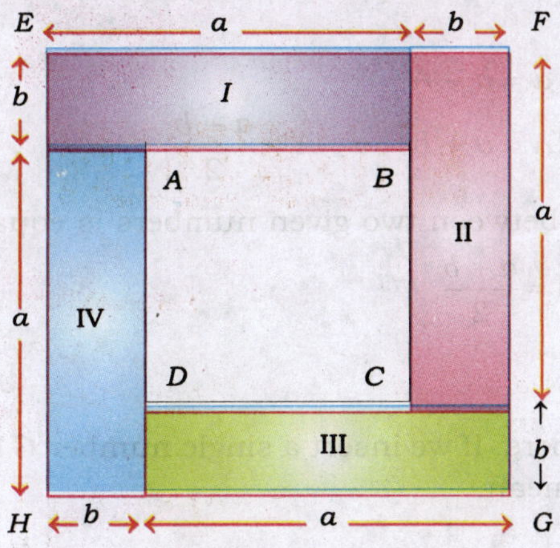

Fig. 13.1

Demonstration

1. $EFGH$ is a square of side $(a + b)$ units.
2. Area $EFGH = (a + b)^2$ sq units.
3. Area of four rectangular pieces $= 4\ (ab) = 4ab$ sq units.
4. $ABCD$ is a square of side $(a - b)$ units.
5. Area $EFGH$ = Sum of the areas of four rectangular pieces + Area of square $ABCD$.

   $\therefore$ Area $EFGH$ > Sum of the areas of four rectangular pieces,

   i.e. $(a + b)^2 > 4\ ab$ or $\left(\frac{a+b}{2}\right)^2 > ab$

   $\therefore\ \frac{a+b}{2} > \sqrt{ab}$, i.e. AM > GM

Observation

Take $a = 5$ cm, $b = 3$ cm

$\therefore$ $EF = a + b =$....... units.

Area of $EFGH = (a + b)^2 =$........ sq units.

Area of each rectangle $= ab =$...... sq units.

Area of square $ABCD = (a - b)^2 =$........ sq units.

Area $EFGH = 4$ (Area of rectangular piece) + Area of square $ABCD$ ...... = 4 (......) + (......)

$\therefore$ (.........) > 4 (.........)

i.e. $(a + b)^2 > 4\,ab$ or $\left(\frac{a+b}{2}\right)^2 > ab$ or $\frac{a+b}{2} > \sqrt{ab}$

$\therefore$ AM > GM

Result

We have learnt that the arithmetic mean of two different positive numbers is always greater than the geometric mean.

Necessary Concepts Related to Activity

1. Arithmetic Mean (AM)

Let a and b be any two numbers and A be a number between them so that a, A, b are in AP, then such a number A is called an arithmetic mean.

Thus, a, A, b are in AP.

$$\therefore \quad A - a = b - A \quad \text{[common difference]}$$

$$\Rightarrow \quad 2A = a + b \Rightarrow A = \frac{a+b}{2}$$

$\therefore$ Arithmetic mean (or average) between two given numbers is equal to half of their sum.

$$\text{AM} = \frac{a+b}{2}$$

2. Geometric Mean (GM)

Let a and b be two positive numbers. If we insert a single number G between them, so that a, G, b is a GP, then G is called geometric mean.

Thus, a, G, b are in GP.

$$\therefore \quad \frac{G}{a} = \frac{b}{G} \Rightarrow G^2 = ab \Rightarrow G = \sqrt{ab}$$

3. Relation between AM and GM

Let A and G be the AM and GM of two positive real numbers a and b, respectively.

Then, $A = \frac{a+b}{2}$ and $G = \sqrt{ab}$

Now, $A - G = \frac{a+b}{2} - \sqrt{ab} = \frac{a+b-2\sqrt{ab}}{2}$

$$\Rightarrow \quad A - G = \frac{(\sqrt{a} - \sqrt{b})^2}{2} \geq 0 \Rightarrow A \geq G$$

Viva-Voce

Q.1 Define arithmetic mean.

Ans Let a and b be any two numbers and A be a number between them so that a, A, b are in AP, then such a number A is called arithmetic mean.

Q.2 What is arithmetic mean between 16 and 20?

Ans Arithmetic mean $= \dfrac{a+b}{2} = \dfrac{16+20}{2} = 18$

Q.3 Write the relation between AM and GM.

Ans AM $\geq$ GM

Q.4 Define the geometric mean.

Ans Let a and b be two positive numbers. If we insert a single number G between them, so that a, G, b is a GP, then G is called geometric mean.

Q.5 The sum of n AM's between a and b is equal to n times the arithmetic mean between a and b. Is it true or false?

Ans True

Q.6 If a and b be two positive numbers and $G_1, G_2, G_3, \ldots, G_n$ be the n GM's between a and b, then $G_n =$ ....

Ans $a\left(\dfrac{b}{a}\right)^{\frac{n}{n+1}}$

Q.7 The product of n GM's between any two positive numbers is equal to nth power of the GM between them. Is it true or false?

Ans True

Q.8 The arithmetic mean between two numbers is 34 and their geometric mean is 16, then the numbers are ....

Ans Let the numbers be a and b.

Then, $\text{AM} = \dfrac{a+b}{2} = 34 \Rightarrow a+b = 68$ ... (i)

Also, $\text{GM} = \sqrt{ab} = 16 \Rightarrow ab = 256$ ... (ii)

Now, $a - b = \sqrt{(a+b)^2 - 4ab} = \sqrt{(68)^2 - 4 \times 256} = 60$

$\therefore \quad a - b = 60$ ... (iii)

From Eqs. (i) and (ii), we get

$$a = 64 \text{ and } b = 4$$

Q.9 The minimum value of $4^x + 4^{1-x}$, $x \in R$ is ....

Ans We have, $\dfrac{4^x + \dfrac{4}{4^x}}{2} \geq \sqrt{4^x \times \dfrac{4}{4^x}}$

[$\because$ AM $\geq$ GM]

$\Rightarrow \quad 4^x + \dfrac{4}{4^x} \geq 2\sqrt{4} \quad \Rightarrow 4^x + \dfrac{4}{4^x} \geq 4$

Q.10 The geometric mean between 3 and $\dfrac{1}{36}$ is ....

Ans Geometric mean between 3 and $\dfrac{1}{36}$ is $\sqrt{3 \times \dfrac{1}{36}} = \sqrt{\dfrac{1}{12}}$

Activity 14

OBJECTIVE

To construct different types of conic sections.

Material Required

Transparent sheet, scissors, cardboard, glue, white sheet.

Prerequisite Knowledge

1. Concept of double napped right circular cone.
2. Concept of conic sections.

Method of Construction

1. Take a cardboard of suitable size and fix a white sheet on it.
2. Cut a transparent sheet in the shape of sector of a circle and fold it to obtain a right circular cone as shown in Fig. 14.1.

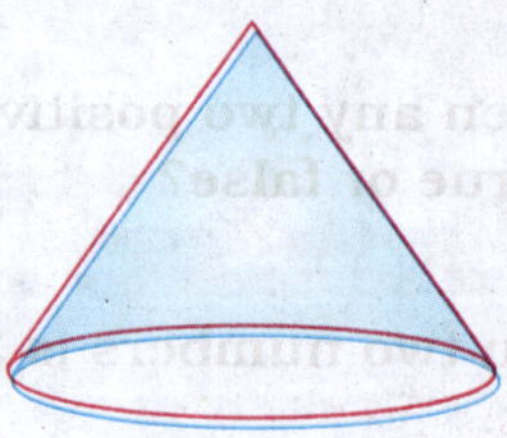

Fig. 14.1

3. Similarly, form four more such cones of the same size using transparent sheet. Put these cones on a cardboard.
4. Now, cut these cones with a transparent plane sheet in different positions as shown in Fig. 14.2 to Fig. 14.5.

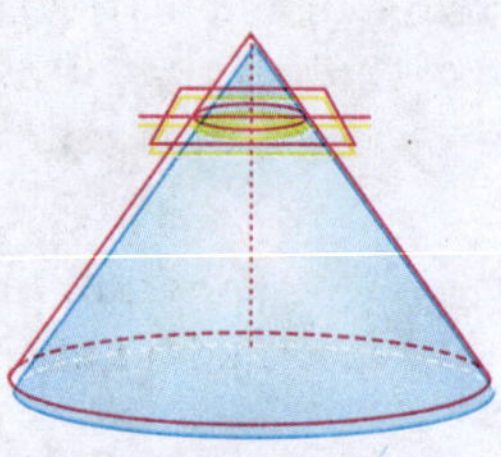

Fig. 14.2

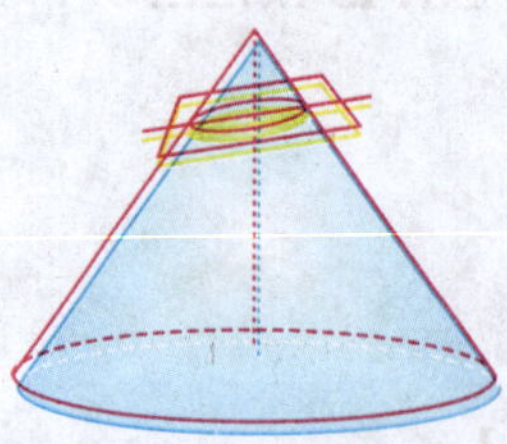

Fig. 14.3

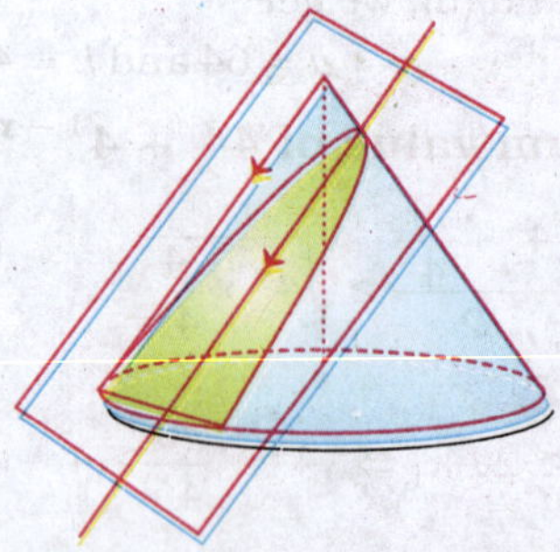

Fig. 14.4

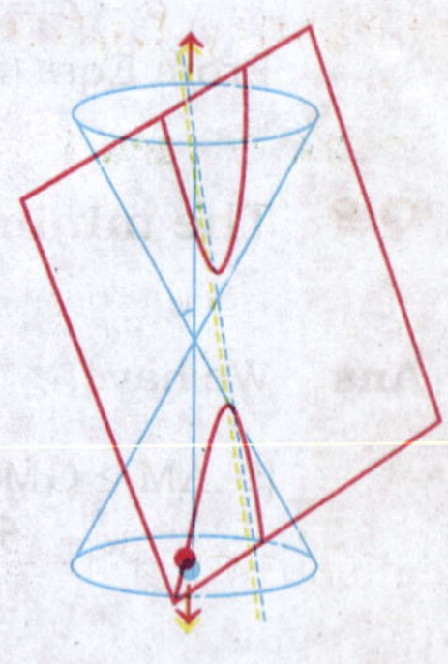

Fig. 14.5

Demonstration

1. In Fig. 14.2, the transparent plane sheet cuts the cone in such a way that the sheet is parallel to the base of the cone. The section so obtained is a circle.
2. In Fig. 14.3, the plane sheet is inclined slightly to the axes of the cone. The section so obtained is an ellipse.
3. In Fig. 14.4, the plane sheet is parallel to a generator (slant height) of the cone. The section so obtained is a parabola.
4. In Fig. 14.5, the plane is parallel to the axis of the cone. The sections so obtained is a part of a hyperbola.

Observation

1. In Fig. 14.2, the transparent plane sheet is .... to the base of the cone.
   The section obtained is ....
2. In Fig. 14.3, the plane sheet is inclined to ....
   The conic section obtained is ....
3. In Fig. 14.4, the plane sheet is parallel to the ....
   The conic section so obtained is ....
4. In Fig. 14.5, the plane sheet is .... to the axis.
   The conic section so obtained is a part of ....

Result

We have learnt how to construct different types of conic section.

Application

This activity helps in understanding various types of conic sections which have wide spread applications in real life situations and modern sciences.

e.g. Conics have interesting geometric properties that can be used for the reflection of light rays and beams of sound, i.e.

1. Circular disc reflects back the light issuing from centre to the centre again.
2. Elliptical disc reflects back the light issuing from one focus to the other focus.
3. Parabolic disc reflects back the light issuing from one focus parallel to its axis.
4. Hyperbolic disc reflects back the light issuing from one focus as if coming from other focus.

Necessary Concepts Related to Activity

1. Double Napped Right Circular Cone

Let AB be a fixed line and l be another line intersecting AB at V and making an angle θ with AB. The locus of the line l is the surface generated by l when it rotates around the line AB so that it always makes an angle θ with AB, is called a double napped right circular cone or cone and extending indefinitely far in both directions.

Here, the fixed line AB is called **axis**, fixed point V is called **vertex** of the cone and the constant angle θ is called the **semi-vertical angle** of the cone. The rotated line l in all its positions is called a **generator** of the cone.

The two parts of the generated surface separated by vertex V are called **nappes.**

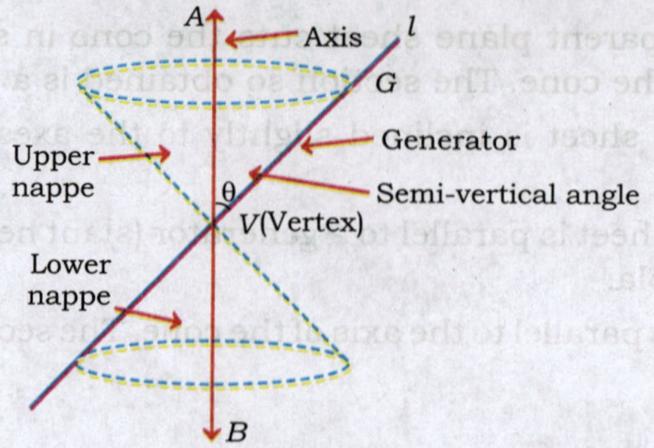

Fig. 14.6

2. Conic Sections

On intersecting a right circular cone by a plane in different positions, different sections so obtained are called conic sections or conics.

Section of a Doubled Napped Right Circular Cone by a Plane

Consider a double napped right circular cone, having semi-vertical angle θ. Let α be the angle between the plane and the axis of cone.

Case I When the plane passes through vertex of the cone

If the plane passes through the vertex of the cone then it cuts both nappes. According to the value of α, we get the following sections:

(a) When $\theta < \alpha \leq 90°$, then the section is a **point**.

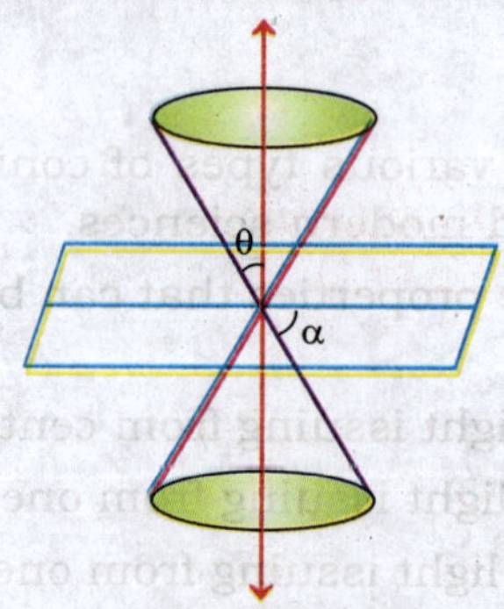

Fig. 14.7

(b) When $\theta = \alpha$, then the plane contains the generator of cone and the section is a **straight line**. It is a **degenerated case of a parabola.**

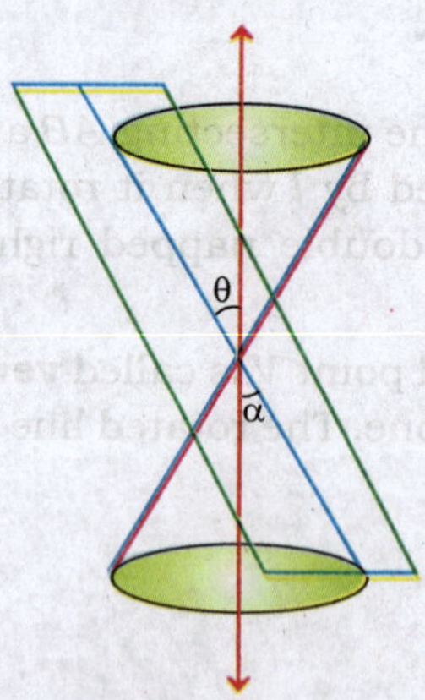

Fig. 14.8

(c) When $0 \leq \alpha < \theta$, then section is a pair of straight lines. It is a **degenerated case of a hyperbola.**

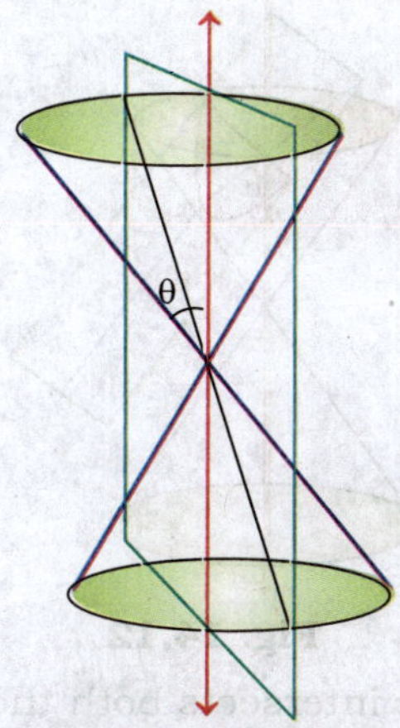

Fig. 14.9

***Case* II When the plane does not pass through vertex of the cone**

If the plane does not pass through the vertex of the cone, then it cuts only one nappe. According to the value of α, we get the following sections:

(a) When $\alpha = 90°$, then cutting plane section is a **circle**.

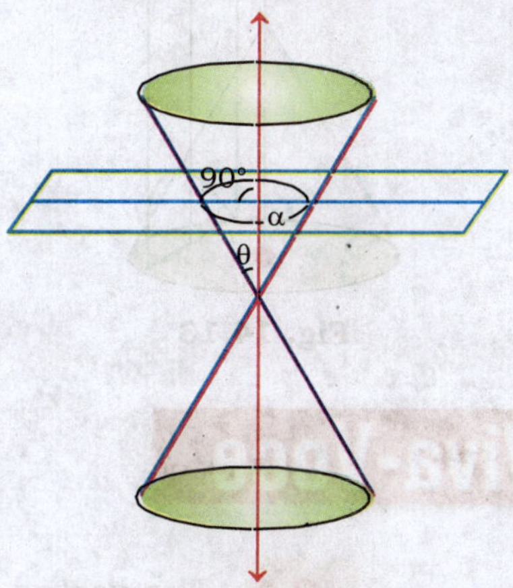

Fig. 14.10

(b) When $\theta < \alpha < 90°$, then cutting plane section is an **ellipse**.

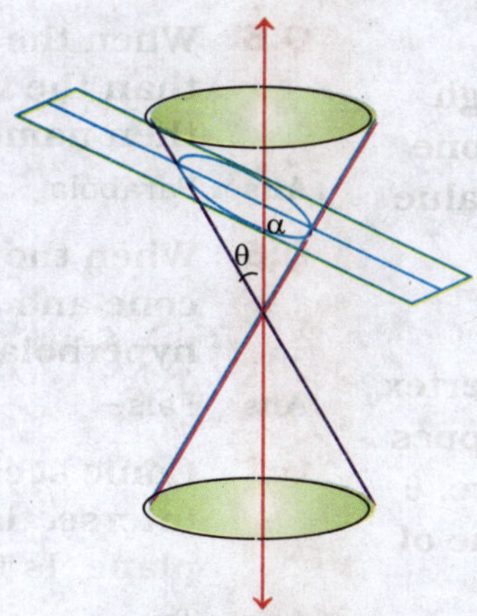

Fig. 14.11

(c) When $\alpha = \theta$, i.e. plane is parallel to a generator, then cutting plane is **parabola**.

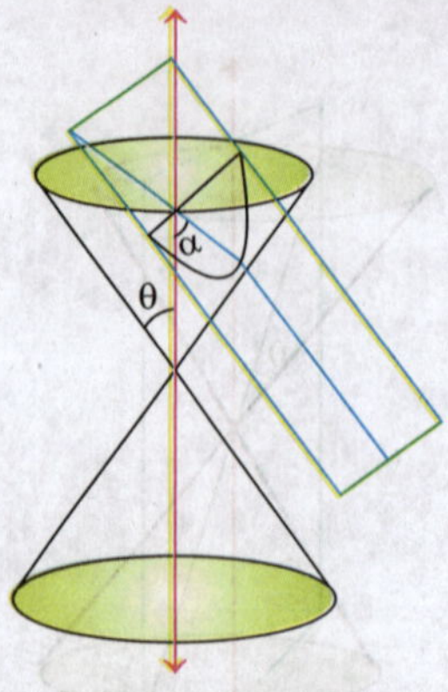

Fig. 14.12

(d) When $0 \leq \alpha < \theta$, then the plane intersects both the nappes and section is a **hyperbola**.

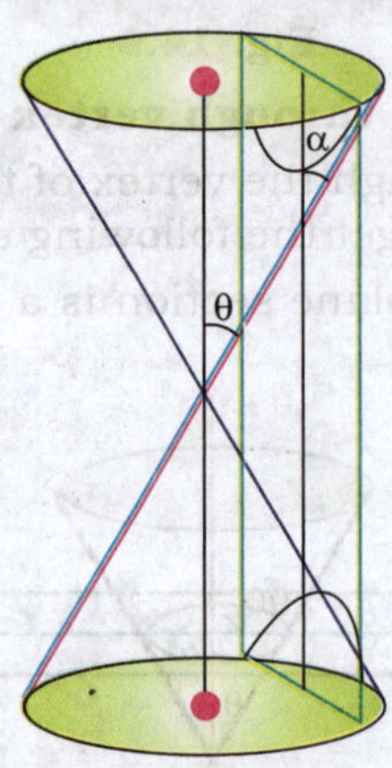

Fig. 14.13

Viva-Voce

Q.1 Define conic section.

Ans When a plane intersects a right circular cone at different positions, then sections so formed are called conic section.

Q.2 When the plane does not pass through vertex of the cone, then it cuts only one nappe at an angle of α, what is the value of α so that conic formed is a circle?

Ans $\alpha = 90°$

Q.3 If the plane does not pass through vertex of the cone, then it cuts both the nappes at an angle of α and if $0 \leq \alpha < \theta$ (where, θ is the semi-vertical angle), then name of section is ....

Ans Hyperbola

Q.4 The vertex separates the cone into two parts called ....

Ans Nappes

Q.5 When the plane cuts the nappes (other than the vertex) of the cone and $\alpha = \theta$, then name of section is ....

Ans Parabola

Q.6 When the plane cuts at the vertex of the cone and $\alpha = \theta$, then name of section is hyperbola. Is it true or false?

Ans False

Q.7 Conic section are the curves obtained by intersecting a right circular cone by a plane. Is it true or false?

Ans True

Activity 15

OBJECTIVE

To construct a parabola.

Material Required

Cardboard, white paper, different coloured pens, compass, ruler etc.

Prerequisite Knowledge

1. Concept of parabola.
2. Concept of standard equations of parabola.

Method of Construction

1. First, take a cardboard of a convenient size and paste a white paper on it.
2. Mark a point S on the white paper on the board (see Fig. 15.1).
3. Through the point S, draw a line. Draw another line l perpendicular to the line through S at some distance λ units to the left of S.

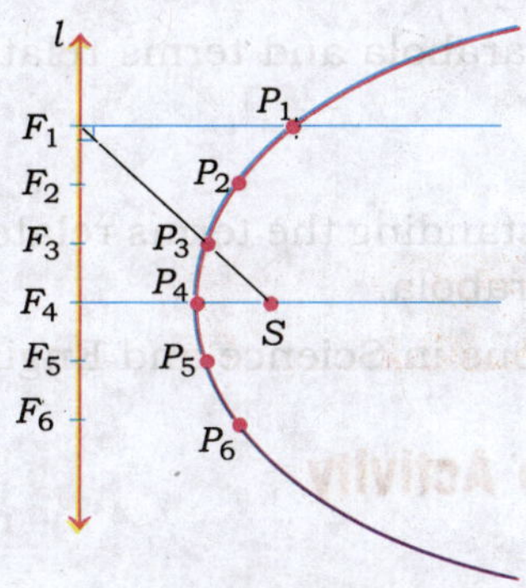

Fig. 15.1

4. Take any point F_1 on the line l. Draw the perpendicular to l at this point.
5. Join F_1S and draw perpendicular bisector of F_1S meeting the perpendicular through F_1 at the point P_1.
6. Take another point F_2 on the line l and repeat the process as explained in Step 5 above to obtain the point P_2.
7. Take some more points F_3, F_4, F_5, ... on the line l and repeat the above process to obtain points P_3, P_4, P_5, ..., respectively.
8. Draw a free hand curve through the points P_1, P_2, P_3, P_4, ... (see Fig. 15.1)

Demonstration

The points P_1, P_2, P_3,...... are such that the distance of each point from the fixed point S is same as the distance of the point from the line l. So, the free hand curve drawn through these points is a parabola with focus S and directrix l.

Observation

1. P_1F_1 = ... P_1S = ...
2. P_2F_2 = ... P_2S = ...
3. P_3F_3 = ... P_3S = ...
4. P_4F_4 = ... P_4S = ...
5. P_5F_5 = ... P_5S = ...
6. The distance of the point P_1 from F_1 = The distance of P_1 from ....
7. The distance between the points P_2 and F_2 = The distance of P_2 from ....

   The distance of the point ...... from F_3 = The distance of the point P_3 from ....
8. Distances of the points P_1, P_2, P_3, ... from the line l are ...... to the distances of these points from the point S.
9. Therefore, the free hand curve obtained by joining P_1, P_2, P_3, ... is a ...... with directrix ...... and focus ....
10. Distance of the vertex P_4 and S = ...
11. Distance of the vertex of parabola from the directrix = ...

Result

We have learnt how to construct a parabola and terms related to it.

Applications

1. This activity is useful in understanding the terms related to parabola, like directrix, focus, property of the point on the parabola.
2. Parabolas have some applications in Science and Engineering.

Necessary Concepts Related to Activity

1. Parabola

A parabola is the locus of a point which moves in a plane such that its distance from a fixed point is always equal to its distance from a fixed straight line in the same plane.

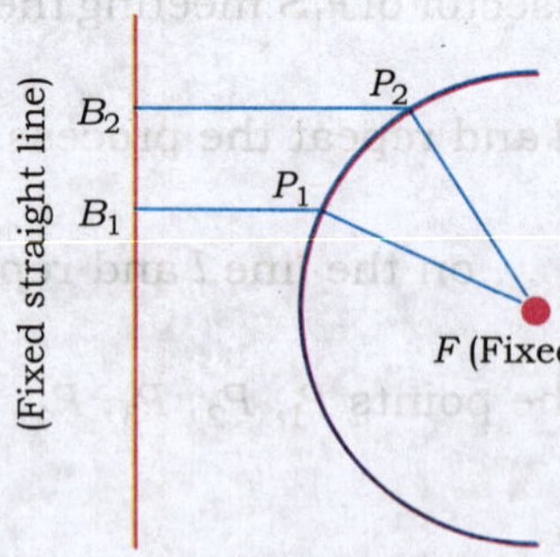

Fig. 15.2

Here, the fixed line is called the **directrix** and the fixed point is called **focus** of the parabola. A line through the focus and perpendicular to the directrix is called the **axis** of the parabola and point of intersection of parabola with the axis is called the **vertex** of the parabola.
In case of parabola, eccentricity (e) is 1.

2. Standard Equations of Parabola

If the equation of the parabola having vertex at origin and the axis of symmetry is either X-axis or Y-axis, then the equations of parabola is said to be in simplest form. There are four standard equations of parabola which are given below.

(i) Right Handed Parabola

If a parabola opens towards right side, then it is called right handed parabola.
The equation of right handed parabola is of the form $y^2 = 4ax, a > 0$

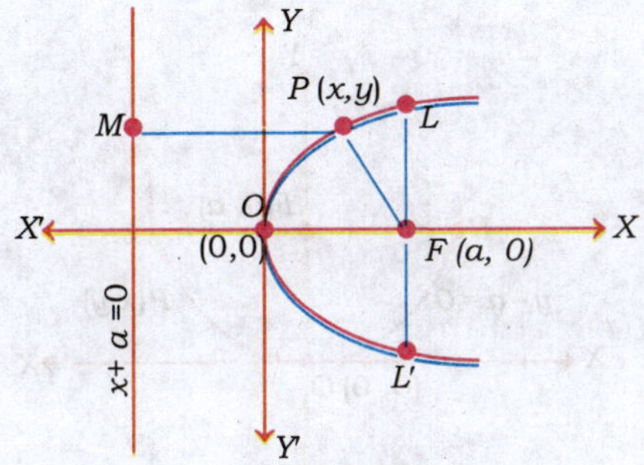

Fig. 15.3

Some terms related to this parabola are

(i) Vertex is O (0, 0).

(ii) Axis is the line $y = 0$.

(iii) Focus is F (a, 0).

(iv) Directrix is the line $x + a = 0$.

(v) Latusrectum of a parabola is a line segment through focus and perpendicular to the axis of the parabola, whose end points lie on the parabola i.e. $LL' = 4a$.

(vi) Equation of latusrectum is $x = a$ or $x - a = 0$.

(vii) It is symmetrical about X-axis.

(ii) Left Handed Parabola

If parabola opens towards left side, then it is called left handed parabola. The equation of the left handed parabola is of the form $y^2 = -4ax, a > 0$

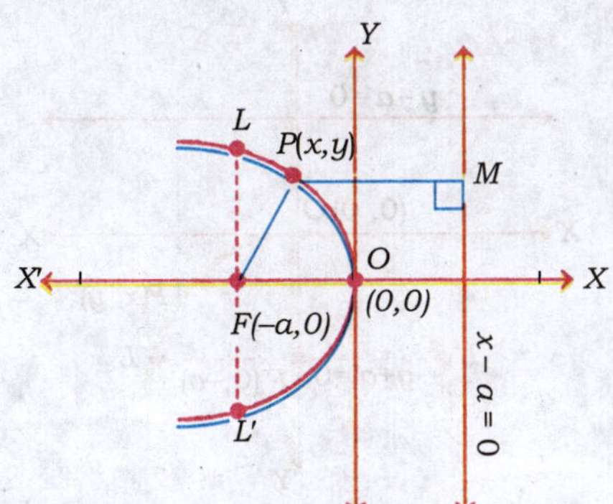

Fig. 15.4

Some terms related to this parabola are

(i) Vertex is $O(0, 0)$.

(ii) Axis is the line $y = 0$.

(iii) Focus is $F(-a, 0)$.

(iv) Directrix is the line $x - a = 0$.

(v) Length of the latusrectum is $4a$.

(vi) Equation of latusrectum is $x = -a$ or $x + a = 0$.

(vii) It is symmetrical about X-axis.

(iii) Upward Parabola

If parabola opens upward, then it is called upward parabola. The equation of the upward parabola is of the form $x^2 = 4ay$, $a > 0$

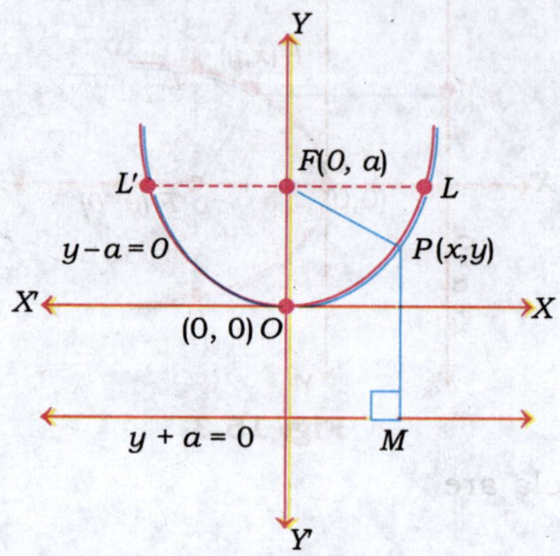

Fig. 15.5

Some terms related to this parabola are

(i) Focus is $F(0, a)$.

(ii) Vertex is $O(0, 0)$.

(iii) Directrix is the line $y + a = 0$.

(iv) Axis is the line $x = 0$.

(v) Length of latusrectum is $4a$.

(vi) Equation of latusrectum is $y = a$ or $y - a = 0$.

(vii) It is symmetrical about Y-axis.

(iv) Downward Parabola

If parabola opens downwards, it is called downward parabola. The equation of downward parabola is of the form $x^2 = -4ay$, $a > 0$

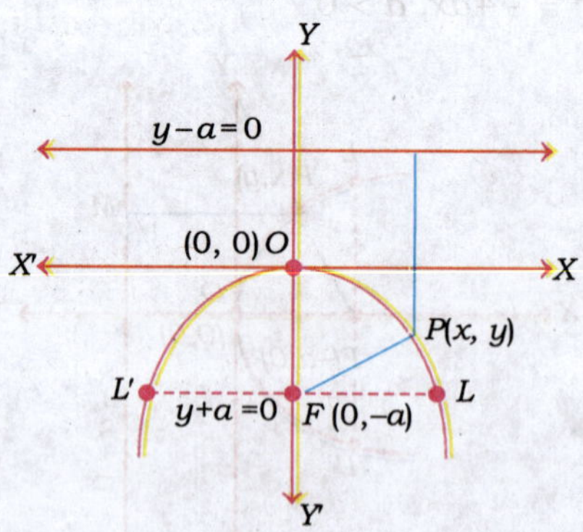

Fig. 15.6

Some terms related to this parabola are

(i) Focus is $F(0, -a)$.

(ii) Vertex is $O(0, 0)$.

(iii) Directrix is the line $y - a = 0$.

(iv) Axis is the line $x = 0$.

(v) Length of latusrectum is $4a$.

(vi) Equation of latusrectum is $y = -a$ or $y + a = 0$.

(vii) It is symmetrical about Y-axis.

Viva-Voce

Q.1 The standard equations of parabolas have focus on one of the coordinates axis, vertex at the origin and the directrix is parallel to the other coordinate axis. Is it true or false?

Ans True

Q.2 Write the axis of the symmetry of the parabola $y^2 = x$.

Ans X-axis.

Q.3 Write the focus of the parabola $x^2 = -4ay$, $a > 0$.

Ans $(0, -a)$

Q.4 'If $e > 1$, then the conic is a parabola', is it true?

Ans No, if $e > 1$, then the conic is a hyperbola. Eccentricity (e) of parabola is 1.

Q.5 Explain about the latusrectum of a conic.

Ans The latusrectum of a conic is the chord passing through the focus and perpendicular to the axis.

Q.6 Explain focal distance.

Ans The distance of a point $P(x, y)$ on parabola from the focus is called focal distance.

Q.7 Write the formula for length of latusrectum of parabola.

Ans $4a$

Q.8 The equation of latusrectum for the parabola $y^2 = -4ax$, $a > 0$ is ....

Ans $x + a = 0$

Q.9 The parabola and point of intersection of parabola with the axis is called the ....

Ans Vertex

Q.10 Describe about the 'parabola'.

Ans A parabola is the locus of a point which moves in a plane such that its distance from a fixed point is always equal to its distance from a fixed straight line in the same plane.

Activity 16

OBJECTIVE

An alternative method of constructing a parabola.

Material Required

Drawing board, white sheet, coloured pens, compasses, ruler, pins, thread.

Prerequisite Knowledge

Refer to Activity 15.

Method of Construction

1. Take a drawing board of a suitable size and fix a white sheet on it.
2. Take any point T on the white sheet fixed on the drawing board.
3. Draw a line through T.
4. Draw another line m perpendicular to the line through T at a distance of k units to the left of T. Let the two lines meet at the point B.

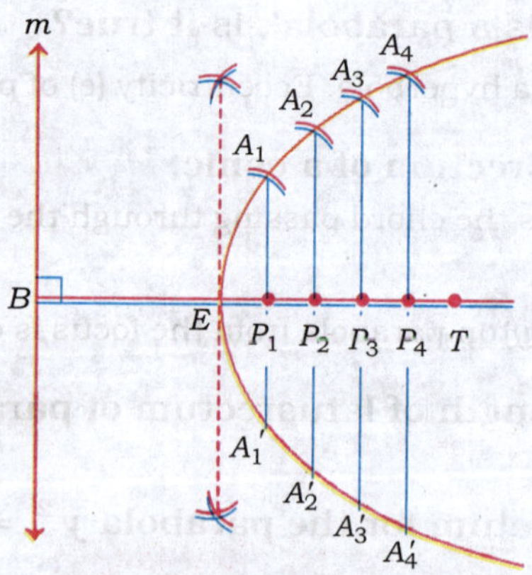

Fig. 16.1

5. Bisect BT at the point E.
6. Mark the points P_1, P_2, P_3 ,.... on ET and draw perpendiculars through these points as shown in the Fig. (16.1).
7. Take T as centre and radius equal to BP_1, draw an arc cutting the perpendicular through P_1 at the point A_1 and A_1'. Similarly, with T as the centre and BP_2 as radius, obtain points A_2 and A_2'. Repeat this process for some more points P_3, P_4, ...and obtain points A_3 and A_3', A_4 and A_4' , ...
8. Fix nails at these points, i.e., A_1, A_2, ..., A_1', A_2', ... and join the foot of the nails by a thread to get a curve as shown in the Fig (16.1).

Demonstration

Distance of the point A_1 from line $m = BP_1 = TA_1$

Similarly, distance of the point A_2 from $m = BP_2 = TA_2$

distance of the point A_3 from $m = BP_3 = TA_3$ and so on.

Also distance of the point A_1' from $m = BP_1 = TA'_1$

distance of the point A_2' from $m = BP_2 = TA_2'$ and so on.

Thus, every point on the curve is equidistant from the line m and the point T. So, the curve is a parabola, with focus T and directrix m.

Observation

By actual measurement

1. Distance of A_1 from line m =...., A_1T = ...
2. Distance of A_2 from line m =...., A_2T = ...
3. Distance of A_3 from line m =...., A_3T = ...
4. Distance of A_4 from line m =...., A_4T = ...
5. Distance of A_1' from line m =...., $A_1'T$ = ...
6. Distance of A_2' from line m =...., $A_2'T$ = ...
7. Distance of A_3' from line m =...., $A_3'T$ = ...
8. Distance of A_4' from line m =...., $A_4'T$ = ...
9. Distance of any point on the curve from line m = Distance of the point from ....
10. So, the curve is .... with directrix .... and focus ....

Result

We have learnt an alternative method for constructing a parabola.

Application

This activity is useful in understanding the terms related to a parabola, such as directrix and focus of the parabola.

Necessary Concepts Related to Activity

Refer to Activity 15.

Viva-Voce

Q.1 Write the equation of a parabola opening upward.

Ans $x^2 = 4ay, a > 0$

Q.2 The coordinates of latusrectum of parabola $y^2 = 4ax, a > 0$ is ....

Ans $(a, \pm 2a)$

Q.3 Write the equation of axis of symmetry of left hand opening parabola.

Ans Equation of given parabola is $y^2 = -4ax$.

$\therefore$ Equation of axis of symmetry is $y = 0$

Q.4 Write the equation of directrix of the parabola $y^2 = 4ax$.

Ans Equation of directrix is $x = -a$

Q.5 What is value of eccentricity of a parabola?

Ans For a parabola, eccentricity $(e) = 1$

Q.6 What is the length of latusrectum of the parabola $ay^2 = 4x$?

Ans Given, parabola is $ay^2 = 4x \Rightarrow y^2 = \frac{4}{a}x$

$\therefore$ Length of latusrectum $= \frac{4}{a}$

Activity 17

OBJECTIVE

To construct an ellipse using a rectangle.

Material Required

A cardboard, white paper, coloured paper, nails, nylon wire/thread, ruler, gum.

Prerequisite Knowledge

1. Concept of ellipse.
2. Concept of standard equation of ellipse.

Method of Construction

1. Firstly, take a rectangular cardboard of a convenient size and paste a white paper on it.
2. After that, cut a rectangle *PQRS* of suitable dimensions from a coloured paper and paste it on the cardboard.
3. Divide this rectangle into four congruent rectangles as shown in the Fig. (17.1).
4. Divide each of the sides *RC* and *DC* of the rectangle *ADCR*, into some equal parts, (say, 11)
5. Mark the point of subdivisions of *RC* as A_1, A_2, ... and that of *DC* as D_1, D_2, ... (see Fig. 17.1)
6. Join the point *A* to points, A_1, A_2, ... and draw the lines joining the point *X* to D_1, D_2, ... (see Fig. 17.1)

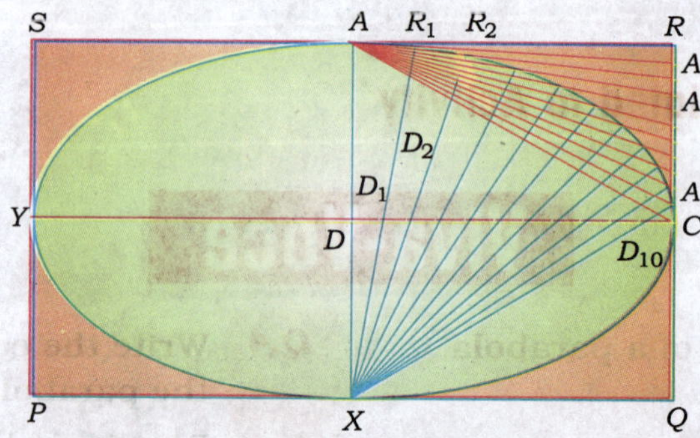

Fig. 17.1

7. Mark the point of intersection of AA_1 and XD_1 as R_1, AA_2 and XD_2 as R_2 and so on.
8. Fix nails at the points R_1, R_2, ..., R_{10}.
9. Join the feet of nails with a nylon wire/thread, as shown in the Fig. (17.1).
10. Repeat the same activity for remaining three congruent rectangles and obtain a curve as shown in Fig. (17.1).

Demonstration

The curve obtained looks like an ellipse. The major axis of this ellipse is the length of the rectangle *PQRS* and the minor axis of the ellipse is the breadth of the rectangle.

Observation

1. Length of the rectangle *PQRS* = ...
2. Breadth of the rectangle *PQRS* = ...
3. Major axis of the ellipse = ...
4. Minor axis of the ellipse = ...

Result

We have learnt how to construct an ellipse using a rectangle.

Application

This activity may be helpful in understanding the concept such as major and minor axis of an ellipse. It is also useful in drawing elliptical designs such as in swimming pools, tables, etc.

Necessary Concepts Related to Activity

1. Ellipse

An ellipse is the locus of a point in a plane which moves in the plane in such a way that the ratio of its distance from a fixed point (called **focus)** in the same plane to its distance from a fixed straight line (called **directrix**) is always constant which is always less than unity.

In other words, we can say that, an ellipse is the set of all points in a plane, the sum of whose distance from two fixed points in the plane is a constant.The two fixed points are called the **foci** (plural of focus) of the ellipse.

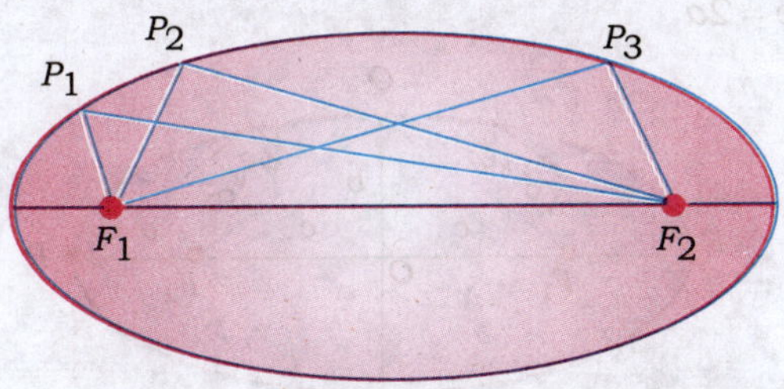

Fig. 17.2

$$P_1F_1 + P_1F_2 = P_2F_1 + P_2F_2 = P_3F_1 + P_3F_2$$

Note The sum of the distances of a point on the ellipse from the two fixed point is always greater than the distance between two fixed points.

2. Definition of Some Terms Related to Ellipse

1. **Centre** The mid-point of the line segment joining the foci is called centre of ellipse.
2. **Major Axis** The line segment through the foci of the ellipse, is called the major axis. The length of major axis is denoted by $2a$.

3. **Minor Axis** The line segment through the centre and perpendicular to the major axis is called minor axis. The length of minor axis is denoted by $2b$.

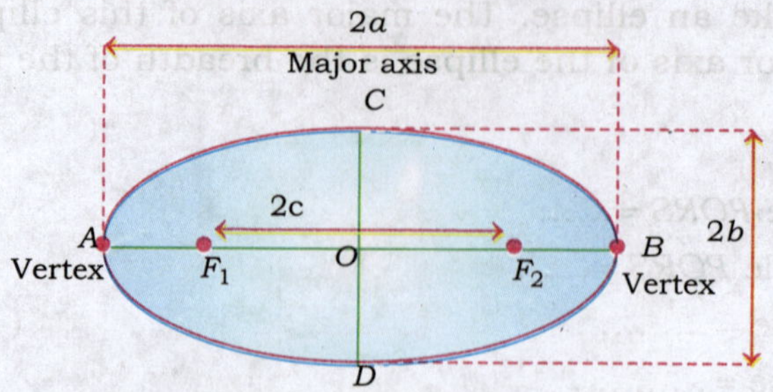

Fig. 17.3

4. **Vertices** The end points of the major axis, are called vertices of the ellipse.
5. **Eccentricity** The eccentricity of ellipse is the ratio of the distances from the centre of the ellipse to one of the foci and to one of the vertices of the ellipse.It is denoted by e.

Thus, $e = \dfrac{c}{a} \Rightarrow c = ae$

Since, $c < a$

$\therefore$ $\dfrac{c}{a} < 1 \Rightarrow e < 1$

3. Relationship between Semi-major Axis, Semi-minor Axis and the Distance of the Focus from the Centre i.e. a, b and c

Let P be a point at one end of major axis.

So, $F_1P = F_1O + OP \Rightarrow F_1P = c + a$ ...(i)

and $F_2P = OP - OF_2 \Rightarrow F_2P = a - c$ ...(ii)

On adding Eqs. (i) and (ii), we get

$$F_1P + F_2P = c + a + a - c = 2a \quad \text{...(iii)}$$

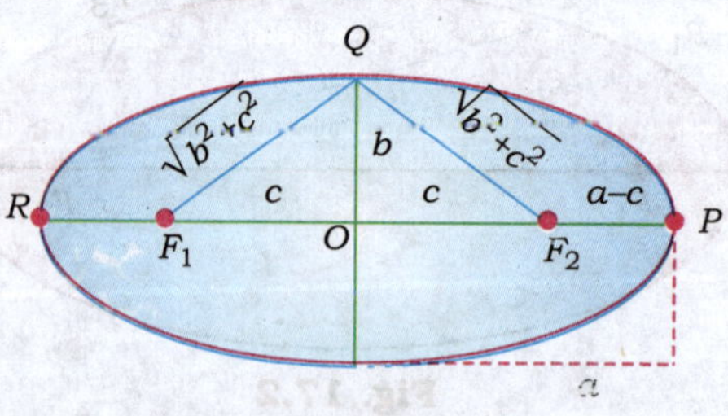

Fig. 17.4

Now, let Q be a point at the end of minor axis. In right angled triangle F_1OQ,

$$F_1Q^2 = OQ^2 + OF_1^2$$

$$\Rightarrow \quad F_1Q^2 = b^2 + c^2$$

$$\Rightarrow \quad F_1Q = \sqrt{b^2 + c^2} \quad \text{...(iv)}$$

Similarly, $F_2Q = \sqrt{b^2 + c^2}$ ...(v)

On adding Eqs. (iv) and (v), we get

$$F_1Q + F_2Q = \sqrt{b^2 + c^2} + \sqrt{b^2 + c^2} \Rightarrow F_1Q + F_2Q = 2\sqrt{b^2 + c^2} \quad \text{...(vi)}$$

From Eqs. (iii) and (vi) and by the definition of the ellipse, we have

$$2\sqrt{b^2 + c^2} = 2a \Rightarrow a = \sqrt{b^2 + c^2} \Rightarrow a^2 = b^2 + c^2 \Rightarrow c = \sqrt{a^2 - b^2}$$

Remark

(i) If $c = 0$, then $a = b$. Thus, ellipse becomes a circle.

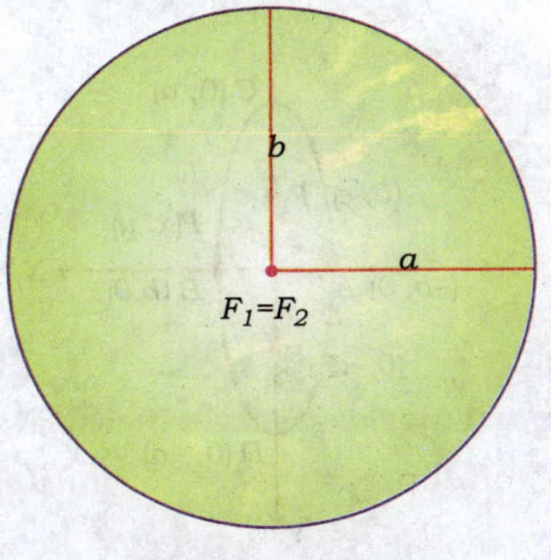

Fig. 17.4 (a)

(ii) If $c = a$, then $b = 0$. Thus, ellipse reduce to line segment $F_1 F_2$.

4. Standard Equation of an Ellipse

(i) Horizontal Ellipse

The standard equation of horizontal ellipse is $\frac{x^2}{a^2} + \frac{y^2}{b^2} = 1, a > b$

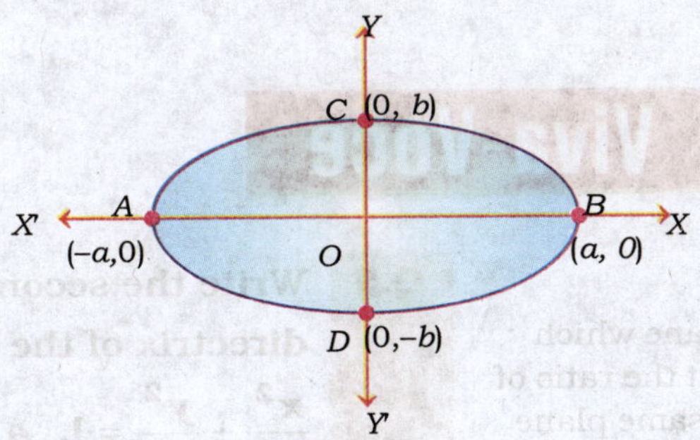

Fig. 17.5

Terms related to horizontal ellipse

(i) Centre is $O(0, 0)$.

(ii) Vertices are $A(-a, 0)$ and $B(a, 0)$.

(iii) Foci are $F_1(-c, 0)$ and $F_2(c, 0)$, where $c = \sqrt{a^2 - b^2}$.

(iv) Length of the major axis, $AB = 2a$.

(v) Length of the minor axis, $CD = 2b$.

(vi) Eccentricity, $e = \frac{c}{a} = \frac{\sqrt{a^2 - b^2}}{a}$.

$\therefore$ **Condition for Horizontal Ellipse** If the denominator of $\frac{x^2}{a^2}$ is greater than the denominator of $\frac{y^2}{b^2}$, then it is a horizontal ellipse and resembles an egg lying on table.

(ii) Vertical Ellipse

The another form of the equation of an ellipse is $\frac{x^2}{b^2} + \frac{y^2}{a^2} = 1$, $a > b$.

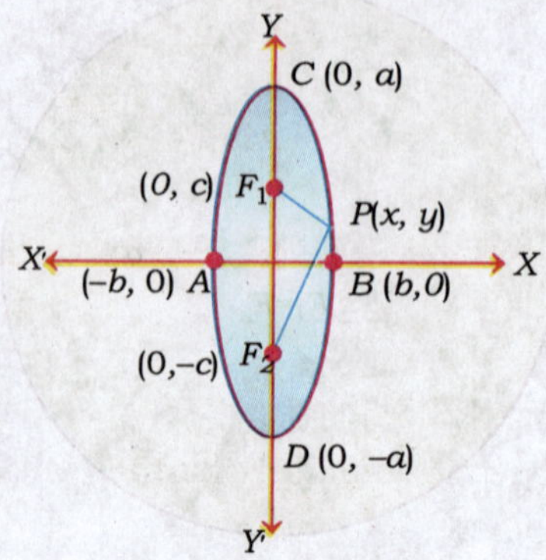

Fig. 17.6

Terms related to vertical ellipse

(i) Centre is $O(0, 0)$.

(ii) Vertices are $C(0, a)$ and $D(0, -a)$.

(iii) Foci are $F_1(0, c)$ and $F_2(0, -c)$.

(iv) Length of the major axis, $CD = 2a$.

(v) Length of the minor axis, $AB = 2b$.

(vi) Eccentricity, $e = \frac{c}{a} = \frac{\sqrt{a^2 - b^2}}{a}$.

$\therefore$ **Condition for Vertical Ellipse** If the denominator of $\frac{y^2}{a^2}$ is greater than the denominator of $\frac{x^2}{b^2}$, then it is a vertical ellipse and resembles an egg standing on table.

Viva-Voce

Q.1 Describe about the 'ellipse'.

Ans An ellipse is the locus of a point in plane which moves in the plane in such a way that the ratio of its distance from a fixed point in the same plane to its distance from a fixed straight line is always constant which is always less than unity.

Q.2 Write the formula of eccentricity to find the eccentricity of the ellipse.

Ans $e^2 = 1 - \frac{b^2}{a^2}$ or $e = \sqrt{1 - \frac{b^2}{a^2}}$

Q.3 If $e < 1$, then the conic is an ellipse, is it true?

Ans Yes, it is true.

Q.4 Write the length of latusrectum for the ellipse $\frac{x^2}{a^2} + \frac{y^2}{b^2}$, $(a < b)$.

Ans $\frac{2a^2}{b}$.

Q.5 Write the second focus and second directrix of the ellipse $\frac{x^2}{a^2} + \frac{y^2}{b^2} = 1$, $a > b$.

Ans Second focus $S'(-ae, 0)$ and second directrix is $x = -\frac{a}{e}$.

Q.6 The distance between foci of an ellipse is $2b$. Is it true or false?

Ans False

Q.7 Write the relation a, b and c.

Ans $c = \sqrt{a^2 - b^2}$

Q.8 If $e = \frac{c}{a}$, then is it true or false?

Ans True.

Activity 18

OBJECTIVE

To construct an ellipse with given major and minor axes.

Material Required

A cardboard, white paper, nylon wire/thread, gum, some chart paper.

Prerequisite Knowledge

Refer to Activity 17.

Method of Construction

1. Take a rectangular sheet of a cardboard of suitable size and fix a white paper on it with the help of gum.
2. Mark a point O on it and draw two concentric circles with centre O whose radii are equal to given semi-major and semi-minor axis of the ellipse. Mark one of the diameter of bigger circle as POQ and call it a horizontal line (see Fig. 18.1).

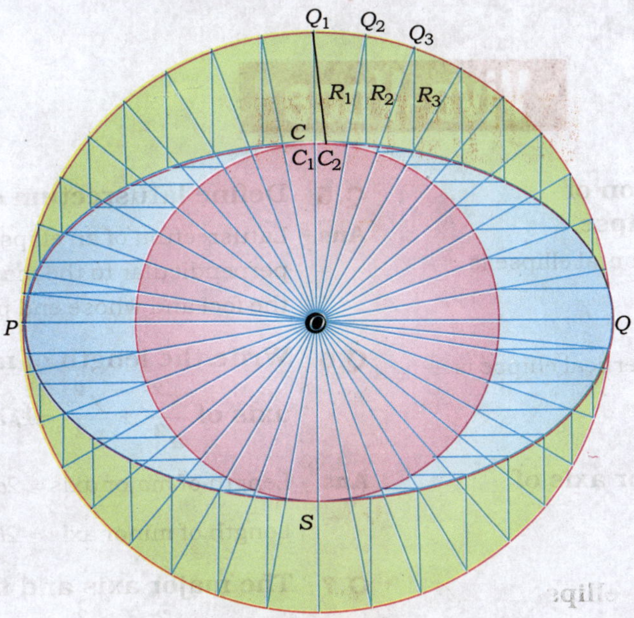

Fig. 18.1

3. Draw radii of the circles in such a way that the angle between two consecutive radii is always same and equal to 10°.
4. Take any radius OQ_1 of the bigger circle cutting the smaller circle at C_1. Draw a horizontal line through C_1 and draw a perpendicular (vertical line) from Q_1 to this horizontal line and obtain point R_1 (see Fig. 18.1).

5. Repeat this process for all the radii OQ_2, OQ_3 and so on of the bigger circle and obtain the points R_2, R_3, ... and so on.
6. Fix the nails at the points R_1, R_2, R_3, ... and join the feet of the nails by a nylon wire/thread and obtain a curve (see Fig. 18.1).

Demonstration

1. The curve obtained looks like an ellipse.
2. Major axis of the ellipse is *POQ* and the minor axis of the ellipse is *COS*, where *COS* is the diameter of the smaller circle perpendicular to diameter *POQ*.

Observation

1. OP =.... and OQ =...
2. OC =... and OS =...
3. Major axis of the ellipse = ..., Minor axis of the ellipse =.....
4. Points R_1, R_2, ... lie on ......

Result

We have learnt how to construct an ellipse with given major and minor axes.

Application

This activity may be used in constructing elliptical designs using thread work and also in explaining concepts such as major and minor axis of an ellipse.

Necessary Concepts Related to Activity

Refer to Activity 17.

Viva-Voce

Q.1 Write the standard equation of horizontal and vertical ellipse.

Ans The standard equation of horizontal ellipse is

$$\frac{x^2}{a^2}+\frac{y^2}{b^2}=1, a>b.$$

And the standard equation of vertical ellipse is

$$\frac{x^2}{b^2}+\frac{y^2}{a^2}=1, a>b$$

Q.2 Write the equation of major axis of $\frac{x^2}{a^2}+\frac{y^2}{b^2}=1$, $a>b>0$.

Ans $y=0$

Q.3 Foci always lie on the major axis of an ellipse. Is it true or false?

Ans True

Q.4 Write the equation of major axis of $\frac{x^2}{b^2}+\frac{y^2}{a^2}=1$, $a>b>0$.

Ans $x=0$

Q.5 Define latusrectum of an ellipse.

Ans Latusrectum of an ellipse is a line segment perpendicular to the major axis through any of the foci and whose end points lie on the ellipse.

Q.6 Write the length of major axis and minor axis of $\frac{x^2}{a^2}+\frac{y^2}{b^2}=1$, $a>b>0$.

Ans Length of major axis = $2a$

Length of minor axis = $2b$

Q.7 The major axis and minor axis of the ellipse $\frac{x^2}{36}+\frac{y^2}{16}=1$ are 12 and 8, respectively. Is it true or false?

Ans True, as here, $a=6$, $b=4$ $\left[\because \frac{x^2}{a^2}+\frac{y^2}{b^2}=1, a>b\right]$

Now, major axis = $2a=2\times6=12$

and minor axis = $2b=2\times4=8$

Activity 19

OBJECTIVE

To construct an ellipse when two fixed points are given.

Material Required

Rectangular cardboard, some coloured chart paper, nails, threads, pen, pencil.

Prerequisite Knowledge

Refer to Activity 17.

Method of Construction

1. Take a rectangular cardboard of suitable size and fix a chart paper on it.
2. Draw a horizontal line on the chart paper and mark two fixed points F_1 and F_2 on it such that the distance between them is 8 cm (say). Fix two nails at the points F_1 and F_2.
3. Take a thread whose length is more than the distance between the two fixed points, 12 cm (say).

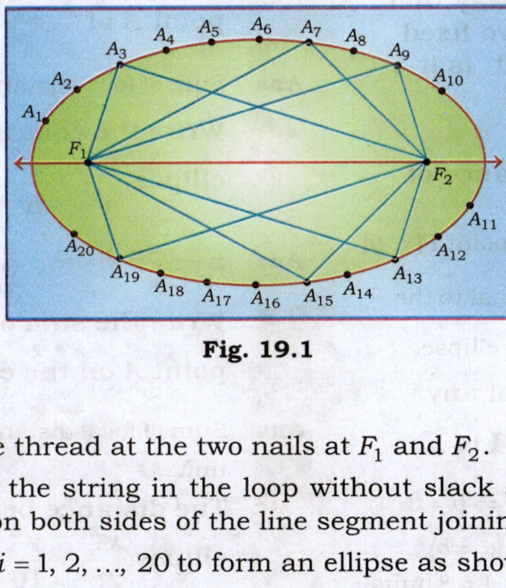

Fig. 19.1

Demonstration

1. Fix the two ends of the thread at the two nails at F_1 and F_2.
2. With a pencil, stretch the string in the loop without slack and mark at least 10 points A_1, A_2, A_3, ..., etc., on both sides of the line segment joining F_1 and F_2.
3. Join all the points A_i, $i = 1, 2, ..., 20$ to form an ellipse as shown in Fig. (19.1).

Observation

1. $A_1F_1 + A_1F_2 = ...$
2. $A_2F_1 + A_2F_2 = ...$
3. $A_3F_1 + A_3F_2 = ...$, $A_4F_1 + A_4F_2 = ...$, $A_6F_1 + A_6F_2 = ...$, $A_9F_1 + A_9F_2 = ...$
4. $A_3F_1 + A_3F_2 = ... + A_4F_2 = A_{19}F_1 + ...$
5. Sum of the distances of each of the points A_1, A_2, A_3, ... from the points F_1 and F_2 is .... So, the curve obtained is an ....

Result

We have learnt how to construct an ellipse when two fixed points are given.

Application

This activity can be used to explain the property of an ellipse, i.e. the sum of the distances of any point on the ellipse from its two foci is constant and is equal to length of major axis.

Note Construct another ellipse by taking different length of the string and also by changing the distance between F_1 and F_2.

Necessary Concepts Related to Activity

Refer to Activity 17.

Viva-Voce

Q.1 If focus is taken as (ae, 0), then corresponding directrix is $x = \frac{a}{e}$ and if focus is (–ae, 0), then corresponding directrix is ....

Ans $x = \frac{-a}{e}$

Q.2 An ellipse is the locus of a point in a plane, which moves in such a way that the sum of its distance from two fixed point in the plane is a constant. Is it true or false?

Ans True

Q.3 Write the sum of the focal distance of any point on the ellipse.

Ans The sum of the focal distance of any point $P(x, y)$ on the ellipse $\frac{x^2}{a^2} + \frac{y^2}{b^2} = 1 (a > b)$ is equal to the length of the major axis, i.e. $2a$ of the ellipse.

Q.4 The sum of the focal distance of any point on the ellipse $\frac{x^2}{16} + \frac{y^2}{9} = 1$ is ....

Ans 8, as given, $a^2 = 16 \Rightarrow a = 4$ and $b^2 = 9 \Rightarrow b = 3$

Therefore, sum of focal distance $= 2a \, (a > b)$

$= 2 \times 4 = 8$ units

Q.5 The sum of the focal distance of any point on the ellipse $\frac{x^2}{25} + \frac{y^2}{144} = 1$ is 24. Is it true or false?

Ans True, as given, $a^2 = 25$

$\Rightarrow \quad a = 5$ and $b^2 = 144 \Rightarrow b = 12$

Therefore, sum of the focal distances $= 2b \, (a < b)$

$= 2 \times 12$

$= 24$ units

Q.6 Write the distance between of two focus of the ellipse $\frac{x^2}{a^2} + \frac{y^2}{b^2} = 1 \, (a > b)$.

Ans Given, equation of ellipse is $\frac{x^2}{a^2} + \frac{y^2}{b^2} = 1 (a > b)$

Let f_1 and f_2 are the two focus, then $f_1 f_2 = 2ae$, where e is the eccentricity.

Q.7 Write the sum of focal distances of a point A of $\frac{x^2}{a^2} + \frac{y^2}{b^2} = 1$, $b > a$.

Ans Sum of focal distances $= 2b$

Q.8 Write the equation of directrix of the ellipse $\frac{x^2}{a^2} + \frac{y^2}{b^2} = 1$, $a > b$.

Ans $x = \pm \frac{a}{e}$, where $e = \sqrt{1 - \frac{b^2}{a^2}}$

Q.9 Write the sum of focal distances of a point A on the ellipse $\frac{x^2}{81} + \frac{y^2}{144} = 1$.

Ans Sum of focal distances $= 2b \, (a < b) = 2 \times 12 = 24$ units.

Q.10 The distance between two focus of the ellipse $\frac{x^2}{25} + \frac{y^2}{16} = 1$ is ....

Ans Given equation of ellipse is $\frac{x^2}{25} + \frac{y^2}{16} = 1$.

Here, $a^2 = 25 \Rightarrow a = 5$ and $b^2 = 16 \Rightarrow b = 4$

$\because a > b$

$\therefore c = \sqrt{a^2 - b^2} = \sqrt{25 - 16} = 3$

$\therefore e = \frac{c}{a} = \frac{3}{5}$

Hence, the distance between of two focus

$= 2ae = 2 \times 5 \times \frac{3}{5} = 6$ Units

Activity 20

OBJECTIVE

To explain the concept of octants by three mutually perpendicular planes in space.

Material Required

A piece of cardboard, saw, wires, rulers wooden-board, paper of different colours, scissors, cutter, thin sheet of wood.

Prerequisite Knowledge

1. Concept of coordinates axes and coordinate planes in three dimensional space.
2. Concept of coordinates of a point in a space.
3. Concept of sign of coordinates.

Method of Construction

1. Take three square sheets each of size 35 cm × 35 cm from a piece of cardboard and fix chart paper of different colours on both sides of sheets.
2. Fix two sheets in such a way that they intersect orthogonally in the middle of each other (see in Fig. 20.1).

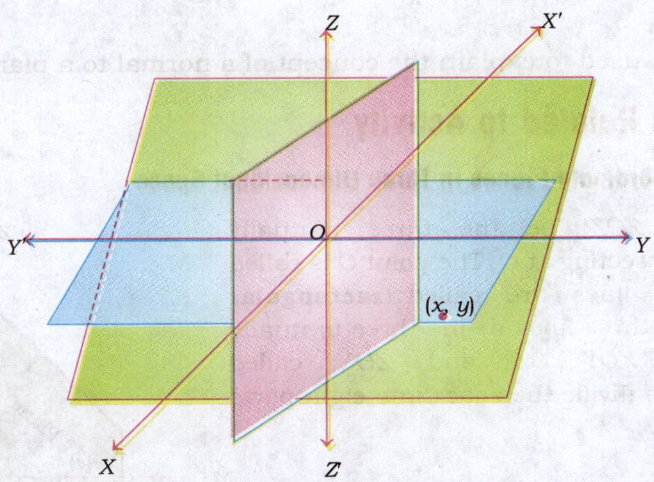

Fig. 20.1

3. Cut the third sheet into two equal rectangles.
4. Insert one rectangle from one side in the middle cutting the two orthogonally, and the other rectangle from the other side (see Fig. 20.1). The space is divided into eight parts by these sheets. Each part is referred to as an octant.
5. Fix the model on a wooden board.
6. In one of the octants, fix rulers to represent *X*-axis, *Y*-axis and *Z*-axis. Extend each of the axis piercing to other sides to represent *XX*′, *YY*′ and *ZZ*′. Mark the point of intersection of *XX*′, *YY*′ and *ZZ*′ as origin *O*.

Demonstration

1. Fix a rod perpendicular to XY-plane at a point $R(x, y)$ and parallel to Z-axis.
2. Fix a wire joining the origin to the upper tip $R'(x, y, z)$ of this perpendicular rod.
3. The distance of point R on XY-plane with coordinates (x, y) from the origin is $\sqrt{x^2 + y^2}$.
4. The distance of R' with coordinates (x, y, z) in space from the origin is

$$\sqrt{(\sqrt{x^2 + y^2})^2 + z^2} = \sqrt{x^2 + y^2 + z^2}$$

Observation

1. The three planes are intersecting at right angles at a point and they divide the space into .... parts. Each part is called an ....
2. Distance of the point (5, 4) on the XY-plane from origin is ....
3. Distance of the point (3, 2, 1) from the origin is ....
4. If we fix a wire perpendicular to any of the planes, then it will represent .... to plane.
5. If two normals are drawn to any two of the planes, then these normals are .... to each other.

Result

We have learnt concept of octants explain by three mutually perpendicular planes in space.

Applications

1. Model can be used to visualise the position and coordinates of a point in space.
2. Model can be used to explain the distance of the origin from a point in the plane or in the space.
3. Model can also be used to explain the concept of a normal to a plane.

Necessary Concepts Related to Activity

1. Coordinate Axes and Coordinate Planes in Three Dimensional Space

Let XOX', YOY' and ZOZ' be the three mutually perpendicular lines, intersecting at O. The point O is called the **origin** and these lines are called **rectangular coordinate axes.** These three lines define three mutually perpendicular planes XOY, YOZ and ZOX called **coordinate planes** which divide the space into eight parts called **octants**.

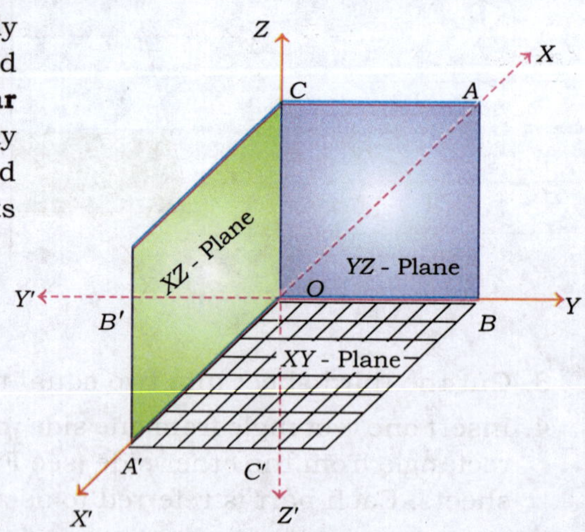

Fig. 20.2

Thus, in the given figure,

$X'OX$ is called the X-axis.

$Y'OY$ is called the Y-axis.

$Z'OZ$ is called the Z-axis.

XOY is called the XY-plane.

YOZ is called the YZ-plane.

ZOX is called the ZX-plane.

$XOYZ$, $X'OYZ$, $XOY'Z$, $X'OY'Z$, $XOYZ'$, $X'OYZ'$, $XOY'Z'$ and $X'OY'Z'$ are called octants.

2. Coordinates of a Point in Space

Let P be a point in space. Through P, draw three planes parallel to the coordinate axes to meet the axes in A, B and C, respectively.

Let $OA = x$, $OB = y$ and $OC = z$. These three numbers taken in order are called **coordinates** of a point P and written as $P(x, y, z)$.

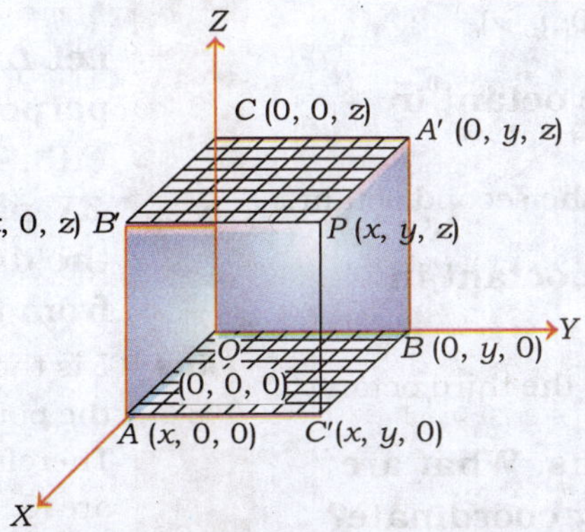

Fig. 20.3

Thus, ***x*-coordinate of a point** P = Length of perpendicular from P to YZ-plane with proper sign.

***y*-coordinate of a point** P = Length of perpendicular from P to ZX-plane with proper sign.

***z*-coordinate of a point** P = Length of perpendicular from P to XY-plane with proper sign.

3. Sign of Coordinates

As we know that, three mutually perpendicular lines $X'OX$, $Y'OY$ and $Z'OZ$ divide the space into eight parts known as octants. Here, OX is the positive direction and OX' is the negative direction of X-axis. Similarly, OY is the positive and OY' is the negative direction of Y-axis and OZ is the positive and OZ' is the negative direction of Z-axis. The sign of coordinates of the points in the eight octants in which the space is divided are given in the following table

Octants / Coordinates	I	II	III	IV	V	VI	VII	VIII
	OXYZ	OX′YZ	OX′Y′Z	OXY′Z	OXYZ′	OX′YZ′	OX′Y′Z′	OXY′Z′
x	+	−	−	+	+	−	−	+
y	+	+	−	−	+	+	−	−
z	+	+	+	+	−	−	−	−

Viva-Voce

Q.1 What are the coordinates of the points lying in the YZ-plane?

Ans The coordinates of the points in the YZ-plane are of the form (0, y, z).

Q.2 Write the name of the octant in which (–4, 2, 5) lies?

Ans The point (–4, 2, 5) lies in the second octant.

Q.3 Write the name of the octant in which (–3, –1, 6) lies?

Ans The point (–3, –1, 6) lies in the third octant.

Q.4 A point is on the Z-axis. What are its x-coordinate and y-coordinate?

Ans Coordinates of any point on the Z-axis is (0, 0, z), because at Z-axis both x and y-coordinates are zero. So its x and y-coordinates are zero.

Q.5 A point in XY-plane, what can you say about its z-coordinate?

Ans When a point is in XY-plane, then its z-coordinate is zero.

Q.6 In the adjoining figure, if the coordinates of point P are (a, b, c), then write the coordinates of A, B and C.

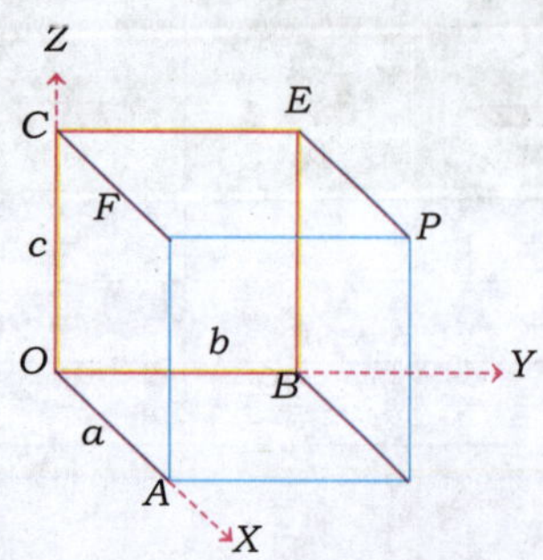

Ans Given, the coordinates of point P are (a, b, c), which shows that OA = a, OB = b and OC = c.

Now, point A lies on X-axis, so its coordinates are (a, 0, 0).

Point B lies on Y-axis, so its coordinates are (0, b, 0) and point C lies on Z-axis, so its coordinates are (0, 0, c).

Q.7 Let L, M, N are the feet of the perpendicular drawn from the point P (3, 4, 5) on the XY, YZ and ZX-planes, respectively. What is the distance of these points L, M, N from the point P?

Ans L is the foot of perpendicular drawn from the point P (3, 4, 5) to the XY-plane. Therefore, the coordinates of the point L are (3, 4, 0). The distance between the points (3, 4, 5) and (3, 4, 0) is 5. Similarly, the lengths of the feet of perpendicular on YZ and ZX-planes and 3 and 4 units, respectively.

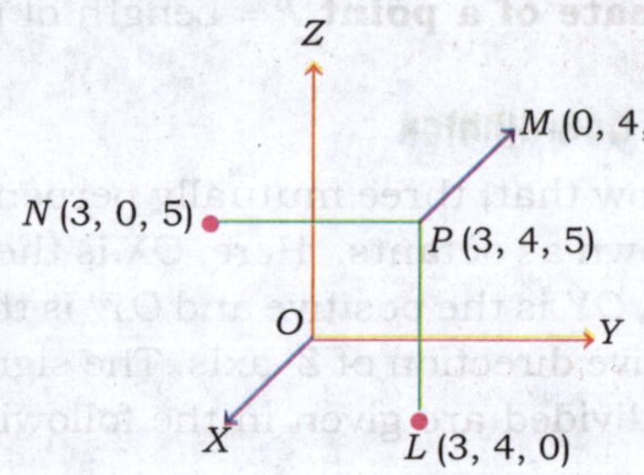

Q.8 If P (x, y, z) is any point in the space, then x, y, z are perpendicular distances from YZ, ZX and XY-planes, respectively. Is it true or false?

Ans True

Q.9 The three coordinate planes divide the space into eight parts known as ....

Ans Octants

Q.10 The sign of the coordinates of a point lying in VII octants is (+, –, +). Is it true or false?

Ans False

Activity 21

OBJECTIVE

To find analytically $\lim_{x \to c} f(x) = \frac{x^2 - c^2}{x - c}$.

Material Required

Pencil, white sheet, calculator.

Prerequisite Knowledge

1. Concept of limit.
2. Concept of left hand limit.
3. Concept of right hand limit.
4. Concept of existence of limit.

Method of Construction

1. Consider the function f given by $f(x) = \frac{x^2 - 16}{x - 4}$.
2. If in this case $c = 4$, then the function is not defined at $x = 4$.

Demonstration

1. Take some values of c less than $c = 4$ and some other values of c more than $c = 4$.
2. In both cases, the values to be taken have to be very close to $c = 4$.
3. Calculate the corresponding values of f at each of the values of c taken close to $c = 4$.

Write the values of $f(x)$ in the following tables

Table 1

x	3.9	3.99	3.999	3.9999	3.99999	3.999999
$f(x)$	7.9	7.99	7.999	7.9999	7.99999	7.999999

Table 2

x	4.1	4.01	4.001	4.0001	4.00001	4.000001
$f(x)$	8.1	8.01	8.001	8.0001	8.00001	8.000001

Observation

1. Values of $f(x)$ as $x \to 4$ from the left, as in Table 1 are coming closer and closer to ....
2. Values of $f(x)$ as $x \to 4$ from the right, as in Table 2 are coming closer and closer to ....

   From Tables (1) and (2), $\lim_{x \to 4} f(x) = \frac{x^2 - 16}{x - 4} =$ ....

Result

We have learnt how to find analytically $\lim_{x \to c} f(x) = \frac{x^2 - c^2}{x - c}$.

Application

This activity can be used to demonstrate the concept of a limit $\lim_{x \to c} f(x)$ when $f(x)$ is not defined at $x = c$.

Necessary Concepts Related to Activity

1. Definition of Limit

If x approaches a, i.e. $x \to a$, then $f(x)$ approaches l, i.e. $f(x) \to l$, where l is a real number, then l is called limit of the function $f(x)$. In symbolic form, it can be written as $\lim_{x \to a} f(x) = l$.

2. Left Hand Limit

A real number l_1 is the left hand limit of function $f(x)$ at $x = a$, if the values of $f(x)$ can be made as close as desired to the number l_1 at point closed to a and on the left of a.

Symbolically, it can be written as LHL = $\lim_{x \to a^-} f(x) = l_1$.

In other words, we can say that $\lim_{x \to a^-} f(x)$ is the expected value of f at $x = a$ given the values of f near x to the left of a. This value is called the left hand limit of $f(x)$ at a.

3. Right Hand Limit

A real number l_2 is the right hand limit of function $f(x)$ at $x = a$, if the values of $f(x)$ can be made as close as desired to the number l_2 at points closed to a and on the right of a.

Symbolically, it can be written as RHL = $\lim_{x \to a^+} f(x) = l_2$.

In other words, we can say that, $\lim_{x \to a^+} f(x)$ is the expected value of f at $x = a$ given the values of f near x to the right of a.

This value is called the right hand limit of $f(x)$ at a.

4. Existence of Limit

If the right hand limit and left hand limit coincide (i.e. same), then we can say that limit exists and that common value is called the limit of $f(x)$ at $x = a$ and it is denoted by $\lim_{x \to a} f(x)$.

Viva-Voce

Q.1 Write the definition of limit.

Ans If x approaches a, i.e. $x \to a$, then $f(x)$ approaches l i.e. $f(x) \to l$, where l is a real number, then l is called limit of the function $f(x)$. In symbolic form, it can be written as $\lim_{x \to a} f(x) = l$.

Q.2 If the left hand limit and right hand limit both exist and coincide, then we can say that limit exists. Is it true or false?

Ans True

Q.3 $\lim_{x \to a^+} f(x)$ is the expected value of f at $x = a$, when we have the values of f near x to the right of a. Is it true or false?

Ans True

Q.4 If f and g be two real functions with common domain D, such that $\lim_{x \to a} f(x)$ and $\lim_{x \to a} g(x)$ exists, then $\lim_{x \to a} [f(x) \cdot g(x)] = \ldots\ldots\ldots$.

Ans $\lim_{x \to a} f(x) \cdot \lim_{x \to a} g(x)$

Q.5 Evaluate $\lim_{x \to 1} \dfrac{x^2 + 1}{x + 100}$.

Ans We have, $\lim_{x \to 1} \dfrac{x^2 + 1}{x + 100} = \dfrac{1^2 + 1}{1 + 100} = \dfrac{2}{101}$

Q.6 Evaluate $\lim_{x \to 3} \dfrac{x^2 - 9}{x + 2}$.

Ans We have, $\lim_{x \to 3} \dfrac{x^2 - 9}{x + 2} = \dfrac{(3)^2 - 9}{3 + 2} = \dfrac{0}{5} = 0$

Q.7 Evaluate $\lim_{x \to 2} (x^4 + 3x^2 + 2)$.

Ans We have, $\lim_{x \to 2} (x^4 + 3x^2 + 2) = (2)^4 + 3(2)^2 + 2$

$$= 16 + 12 + 2 = 30$$

Q.8 $\lim_{x \to \frac{1}{2}} \dfrac{4x^2 - 1}{2x - 1} = \ldots\ldots\ldots$

Ans 2, as $\lim_{x \to \frac{1}{2}} \dfrac{4x^2 - 1}{2x - 1} = \lim_{x \to \frac{1}{2}} \dfrac{(2x + 1)(2x - 1)}{(2x - 1)}$

$$= \lim_{x \to \frac{1}{2}} (2x + 1) = 2\left(\frac{1}{2}\right) + 1 = 2$$

Q.9 Evaluate $\lim_{x \to 2} \left[\dfrac{x^2 - 4}{x^3 - 4x^2 + 4x}\right]$.

Ans On putting the limit i.e. at $x = 2$, we get the form $\dfrac{0}{0}$

$$\therefore \lim_{x \to 2} \frac{x^2 - 4}{x^3 - 4x^2 + 4x} = \lim_{x \to 2} \frac{(x + 2)(x - 2)}{x(x - 2)^2}$$

$$= \lim_{x \to 2} \frac{(x + 2)}{x(x - 2)} = \frac{2 + 2}{2\,(2 - 2)} = \frac{4}{0}$$

which is not defined.

Q.10 $\lim_{x \to 3} (x^2 - 9)\left(\dfrac{1}{x + 3} + \dfrac{1}{x - 3}\right) = 5$. Is it true or false?

Ans False,

We have, $\lim_{x \to 3} (x^2 - 9)\left(\dfrac{1}{x + 3} + \dfrac{1}{x - 3}\right)$

$$= \lim_{x \to 3} (x + 3)(x - 3)\left[\frac{x - 3 + x + 3}{(x + 3)(x - 3)}\right]$$

$$= \lim_{x \to 3} (2x) = 2 \times 3 = 6$$

Activity 22

OBJECTIVE

Verification of the geometrical significance of derivative.

Material Required

Graph sheets, glue, hardboard, trigonometric tables, geometry box, wires.

Prerequisite Knowledge

1. Concept of geometrical interpretation of derivative of a function at a point.
2. Concept of first principle of derivative.

Method of Construction

1. Firstly, paste three graph sheets on a hardboard and draw two mutually perpendicular lines representing X-axis and Y-axis on each of them.
2. Sketch the graph of the curve (circle) $x^2 + y^2 = 25$ on first graph sheet.

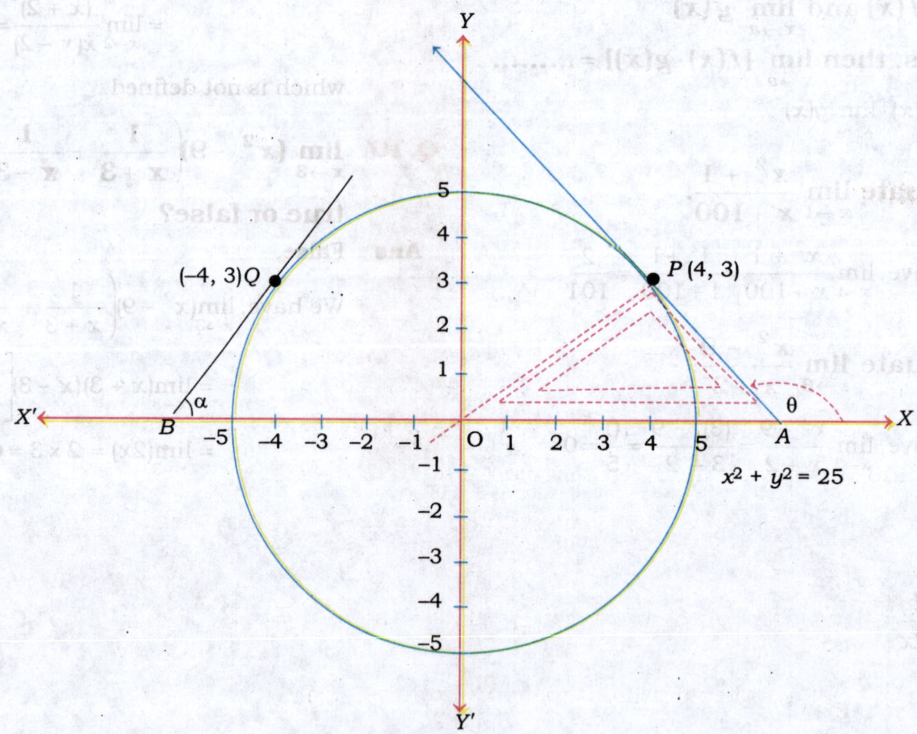

Fig. 22.1

3. Similarly, sketch the graphs of $(x-3)^2 + y^2 = 25$ and the curve $xy = 4$ (rectangular hyperbola) on the other graph sheets.

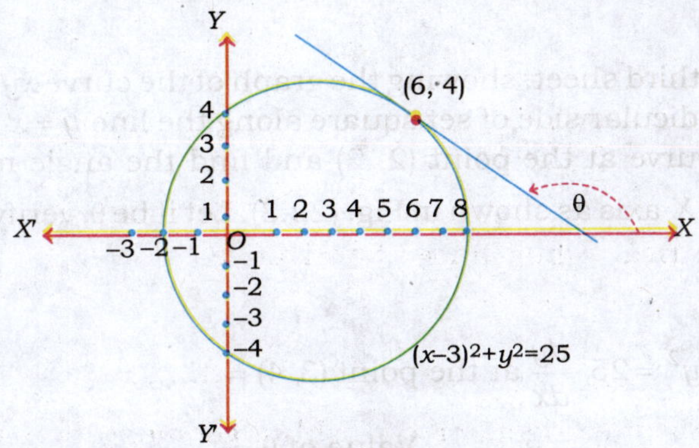

Fig. 22.2

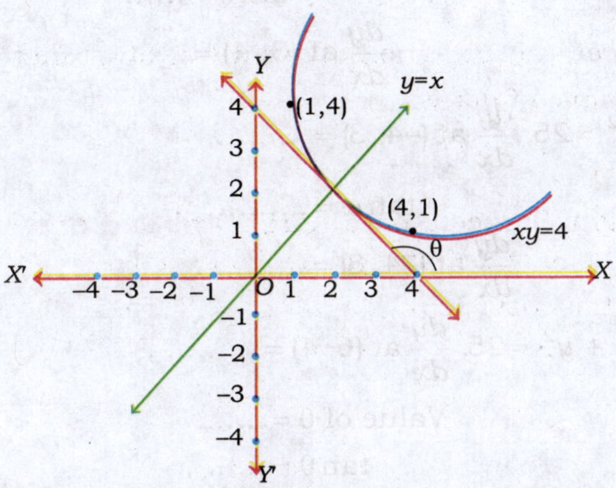

Fig. 22.3

Demonstration

1. Firstly, take first sheet on which, the graph of the circle $x^2 + y^2 = 25$ has been drawn (see Fig. 22.1)
2. Take a point $P(4, 3)$ on the circle.
3. With the help of a set square, place a wire in the direction OP and other perpendicular to OP at the point P to meet X-axis at a point (say A).
4. Measure the angle between the wire and the positive direction of X-axis at A (say θ).
5. Then, find $\tan\theta$ (with the help of trigonometric tables).

   Now, $x^2 + y^2 = 25 \Rightarrow y = \sqrt{25 - x^2} \Rightarrow \frac{dy}{dx} = \frac{-x}{\sqrt{25 - x^2}}$.

   Find $\frac{dy}{dx}$ at the point (4, 3) and verify that $\left(\frac{dy}{dx}\right)$ at $(4, 3) = \tan\theta$.

6. Similarly, take another point (–4, 3) on the circle. Verify that $\frac{dy}{dx}$ at $(-4, 3) = \tan\alpha$, where α is the angle made by the tangent to the circle at the point (–4, 3) with the positive direction of X-axis. (see Fig. (22.1)).

7. Take other sheet with the graph of $(x-3)^2+y^2=25$ and take the point (6, 4) on it and repeat the above process using set square and wires as shown in Fig. (22.2) i.e. verify that $\frac{dy}{dx}$ at (6, 4) = $\tan\theta$.
8. In the end, take the third sheet, showing the graph of the curve $xy=4$. Take the point (2, 2) on it. Place one perpendicular side of set square along the line $y=x$ and a wire along the other side touching the curve at the point (2, 2) and find the angle made by the wire with the positive direction of X-axis as shown in Fig. (22.3). Let it be θ, verify that $\frac{dy}{dx}$ at (2, 2) = $\tan\theta$.

Observation

1. For the curve $x^2+y^2=25$, $\frac{dy}{dx}$ at the point (3, 4) = ...,

   Value of θ = ...,

   $\tan\theta$ = ...

   $\frac{dy}{dx}$ at (3, 4) = ...

2. For the curve $x^2+y^2=25$, $\frac{dy}{dx}$ at (–4, 3) = ...,

   $\tan\alpha$ = ...,

   $\frac{dy}{dx}$ at (–4, 3) = ...

3. For the curve $(x-3)^2+y^2=25$, $\frac{dy}{dx}$ at (6, 4) = ... ,

   Value of θ = ...,

   $\tan\theta$ = ... ,

   $\frac{dy}{dx}$ at (6, 4) = ... ,

4. For the curve $xy=4$, $\left(\frac{dy}{dx}\right)$ at (2, 2) = ... ,

   θ = ...,

   $\tan\theta$ = ...

Result

We have learnt how to verified the geometrical significance of derivative.

Application

This activity can be used to verify the result that the slope of the tangent at a point is equal to the value of the derivative at that point for other curves.

Note *The activity may be repeated by taking point (4, 3) on first sheet, (0, 4) on second sheet and (1, 4) on the third sheet.*

Necessary Concepts Related to Activity

1. Geometrical Interpretation of Derivative of a Function at a Point

Let $y = f(x)$ be a continuous function and let $P[a, f(a)]$ and $Q[(a + h), f(a + h)]$ be two points close to each other on the graph of this function as shown in Fig. (22.4).

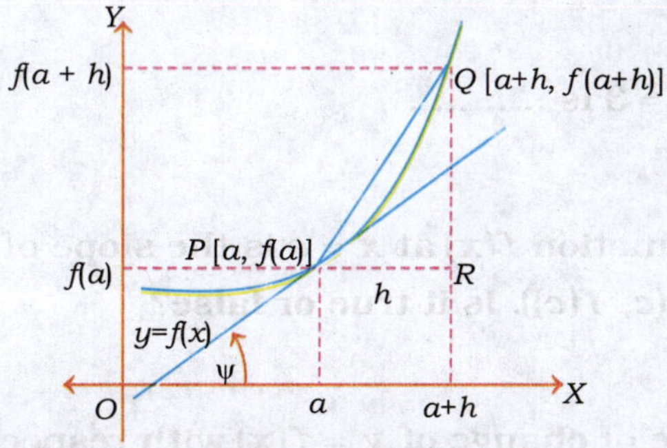

Fig. 22.4

Now, in ΔPQR, $\tan \angle QPR = \dfrac{QR}{PR}$.

It is clear that, this ratio is precisely equal to $\tan \angle QPR$, which is the slope of the chord PQ.

We know that, $f'(a) = \lim\limits_{h \to 0} \dfrac{f(a+h) - f(a)}{h}$

On taking limit $h \to 0$, the point $Q \to P$

and we have $\lim\limits_{h \to 0} \dfrac{f(a+h) - f(a)}{h} = \lim\limits_{Q \to P} \dfrac{QR}{PR}$

This is equivalent to the fact that, the chord PQ tends to the tangent at P of the curve $y = f(x)$. Thus, the limit turns out to be equal to the slope of the tangent. i.e. $f'(a) = \tan \Psi$.

2. First Principle of Derivative

Suppose f is a real valued function, the function defined by $\lim\limits_{h \to 0} \dfrac{f(x+h) - f(x)}{h}$, wherever the limit exists is defined to be the derivative of f at x and is denoted by $f'(x)$. This definition of derivative is called the first principle of derivative.

Thus, $f'(x) = \lim\limits_{x \to 0} \dfrac{f(x+h) - f(x)}{h}$

Sometimes $f'(x)$ is denoted by $\dfrac{d}{dx}[f(x)]$ or if $y = f(x)$, then it is denoted by $\dfrac{dy}{dx}$ and referred to as derivative of $f(x)$ or y with respect to x. It is also denoted by $D[f(x)]$.

Viva-Voce

Q.1 $f'(a) = \lim_{h \to 0} \frac{f(a+h) - f(a)}{h}$. **Is it true or false?**

Ans True

Q.2 **For** $f(x) = 3$, $\frac{dy}{dx}$ **at** $x = 3$ **is ....**

Ans 0

Q.3 **The derivative of a function** $f(x)$ **at** $x = c$ **is the slope of the tangent to the curve** $y = f(x)$ **at the point** $(c, f(c))$**. Is it true or false?**

Ans True

Q.4 $\frac{dy}{dx}$ **measures the rate of change of** $y = f(x)$ **with respect to ....**

Ans x

Q.5 $\frac{dy}{dx} = \lim_{\Delta x \to 0} \frac{\Delta y}{\Delta x}$. **Is it true or false?**

Ans True

Q.6 $\frac{d}{dx}(x^n) = nx^{n-1}$. **Is it true or false?**

Ans True.

Q.7 **Write the derivative of** $\sqrt{x}$.

Ans $\frac{d}{dx}(\sqrt{x}) = \frac{1}{2\sqrt{x}}$

Q.8 **Write the derivative of** $\sin x$.

Ans $\cos x$

Q.9 $\frac{d}{dx}(\cos x) = \sin x$. **Is it true or false?**

Ans False.

Q.10 **The slope of tangent to the curve** $y = x^2$ **at** $\left(-\frac{1}{2}, \frac{1}{4}\right)$ **is ....**

Ans -1, as $\frac{dy}{dx} = 2x$

$\therefore \left(\frac{dy}{dx}\right)_{\left(-\frac{1}{2}, \frac{1}{4}\right)} = 2\left(-\frac{1}{2}\right) = -1$

Activity No. ____________ Date ________ Page No. ________

Teacher Signature ________________

Activity No. ____________ Date ________ Page No. ________

Teacher Signature ________________

Activity No. ________ Date ________ Page No. ________

Teacher Signature ________

Activity No. ________ Date ________ Page No. ________

Teacher Signature ________

Activity No. ____________ Date ________ Page No. ________

Teacher Signature ____________________

Activity No. ____________ Date ________ Page No. ________

Teacher Signature ________________

Activity No.__________ Date _______ Page No. _______

Teacher Signature_______________

Activity No.__________ Date ________ Page No. ________

Teacher Signature________________

Activity No. ____________ Date ________ Page No. ________

Teacher Signature ________________

Activity No. ____________ Date ________ Page No. ________

Teacher Signature________________

Activity No. ____________ Date ________ Page No. ________

Teacher Signature ________________

Activity No. ___________ Date ________ Page No. ________

Teacher Signature ________________

Activity No. ____________ Date ________ Page No. ________

Teacher Signature ________________

Activity No.____________ Date ________ Page No. ________

Teacher Signature____________

Activity No. ____________ Date ________ Page No. ________

Teacher Signature ________________

Activity No. ______ Date ______ Page No. ______

Teacher Signature ______

Activity No. ____________ Date ________ Page No. ________

Teacher Signature ____________________

Activity No. ____________ Date ________ Page No. ________

Teacher Signature ________________

Activity No. ___________ Date ________ Page No. ________

Teacher Signature ______________

Activity No. ____________ Date ________ Page No. ________

Teacher Signature ________________

Activity No. ____________ Date ________ Page No. ________

Teacher Signature ________________

Activity No. __________ Date ________ Page No. ________

Teacher Signature ______________

Activity No. ____________ Date ________ Page No. ________

Teacher Signature________________

Activity No. ____________ Date __________ Page No. __________

Teacher Signature ________________

Activity No. ____________ Date ________ Page No. ________

Teacher Signature ________________

Activity No. ____________ Date ________ Page No. ________

Teacher Signature ________________

Activity No. ____________ Date ________ Page No. ________

Teacher Signature ________________

Activity No. ___________ Date ________ Page No. ________

Teacher Signature_______________

Activity No. ___________ Date ________ Page No. ________

Teacher Signature ________________

Activity No. ____________ Date ________ Page No. ________

Teacher Signature ________________

Activity No. ____________ Date ________ Page No. ________

Teacher Signature ________________

Activity No. ___________ Date ________ Page No. ________

Teacher Signature ________________

Activity No. ___________ Date ________ Page No. ________

Teacher Signature ______________

Activity No. ___________ Date ________ Page No. ________

Teacher Signature ________________

Activity No. ___________ Date ________ Page No. ________

Teacher Signature _______________

Activity No. __________ Date ________ Page No. ________

Teacher Signature ____________

Activity No. ___________ Date ________ Page No. ________

Teacher Signature _______________

Activity No. ____________ Date ________ Page No. ________

Teacher Signature ________________

Activity No. ____________ Date ________ Page No. ________

Teacher Signature ________________

Activity No. ____________ Date ________ Page No. ________

Teacher Signature________________

Activity No. ____________ Date ________ Page No. ________

Teacher Signature ________________

Activity No.__________ Date _______ Page No. _______

Teacher Signature____________

Activity No. ________ Date ______ Page No. ______

Teacher Signature ____________

Activity No. ____________ Date ________ Page No. ________

Teacher Signature ________________

Activity No.__________ Date _______ Page No. _______

Teacher Signature______________

Activity No. __________ Date ________ Page No. ________

Teacher Signature ____________

Activity No. ____________ Date ________ Page No. ________

Teacher Signature ________________

Activity No. ___________ Date ________ Page No. ________

Teacher Signature_______________

Activity No. __________ Date _______ Page No. _______

Teacher Signature ______________

Activity No. ________ Date ________ Page No. ________

Teacher Signature ________

Activity No. ________ Date ________ Page No. ________

Teacher Signature ________

Activity No. ___________ Date ________ Page No. ________

Teacher Signature ________________

Activity No. ____________ Date ________ Page No. ________

Teacher Signature ________________

Activity No. ____________ Date ________ Page No. ________

Teacher Signature ________________

Activity No. ____________ Date ________ Page No. ________

Teacher Signature________________

Activity No. ________ Date ________ Page No. ________

Teacher Signature ________

Activity No. ___________ Date ________ Page No. ________

Teacher Signature ________________

Activity No. __________ Date ________ Page No. ________

Teacher Signature ______________

Activity No. __________ Date ________ Page No. ________

Teacher Signature ______________

Activity No. ________ Date ________ Page No. ________

Teacher Signature ________

Activity No. ____________ Date ________ Page No. ________

Teacher Signature ________________

Activity No.__________ Date ________ Page No. ________

Teacher Signature______________

Activity No. ____________ Date ________ Page No. ________

Teacher Signature ________________

Activity No. ____________ Date ________ Page No. ________

Teacher Signature ________________